Polenta on the Board

Cara Miriam,

Thank you for helping
to share Nonna Sofia's
legacy. She would have
loved to know you.
Buon appetito!

Valerie

May 2/03

Polenta on the Board

Italian family cooking, Abruzzese style

VALERIE MITCHELL

Foreword by author, editor and TV Host
STAR WEISS FUOCO

TEXT: Valerie Mitchell
EDITOR: Lindsay Sovran Mitchell
BOOK DESIGN AND PRODUCTION: Miriam MacPhail
PHOTOGRAPHIC CONSULTANT: Dante Poscente
    Photograph on page 3 courtesy Star Weiss Fuoco.
    All other photos generously made available by
    family members: Dante Poscente, Julio Poscente,
    Eleanor Sovran, Bruce Mitchell, Alison Mitchell,
    Lorraine Sovran Taylor.
PRINTED BY: Morriss Printing Co. Ltd., Victoria, BC Canada

Valerie Mitchell
1619 Hollywood Crescent
Victoria, British Columbia
Canada V8S 1H8

Website: http://members.shaw.ca/polenta
Email: polenta@shaw.ca

Author's note: A number of references are made to the Abruzzo region of Italy. The region is also often referred to as 'Abruzzi' on maps and in publications about the area.

National Library of Canada
Cataloguing in Publication Data:
Mitchell, Valerie, 1951–
    Polenta on the board : Italian family cooking,
    Abruzzese-style / Valerie Mitchell.

    Includes some text in Italian.
    Includes bibliographical references and index.
    ISBN 0-9732851-0-9

    1. Cookery, Italian.
    2. Cookery–Italy–Abruzzo. I. Title.
TX723.2.S65M59 2003   641.5945'71
C2003-910575-X

Dedication

For Nonna Sofia and Papa Vincenzo Poscente

who raised their family with love and instilled in us a pride in our roots

and for their children,

Antonio (and Mary), Dante (and Lucy), Eleanor (and Attilio),

Julio (and Maureen) and Ernesto (and Patricia)

who carried on these traditions

In Appreciation

Just as growing, harvesting, preparing and sharing the food for these dishes relied on a collective effort, so too did the preparation of this cookbook. I would like to express my appreciation to everyone who helped:

❖ My parents, aunts and uncles, sister and brother, cousins and relatives who contributed recipes and photographs and shared their stories

❖ My husband and our daughters who provided me support, encouragement and advice as the project progressed

❖ Friends and family who were willing taste testers and helped with marketing and distribution

❖ All of the volunteers who offered their services as test kitchens for each recipe and provided invaluable feedback

❖ My cookbook-aficionado friends who shared their preferences for layout and design

❖ Dawn Roberts who guided me in the creation of an index and table of contents and participated in a final edit of the manuscript

❖ Editor, Lindsay Sovran Mitchell, whose advice and feedback was invaluable and always constructively conveyed

❖ Photography advisor, Dante Poscente, who provided guidance and advice in the collection, selection and presentation of photographs

❖ Book designer, Miriam MacPhail, who took a personal interest in the stories and recipes and who brought creativity and professionalism to their presentation

❖ Star Weiss Fuoco whose invaluable assistance and good-natured guidance reflected her unswerving commitment to quality assurance.

Table of Contents

The Soup Pot   11

Polenta on the board   24

Table of Contents

Continued

Fish on Fridays 59

The ovens of Antrodoco 105

Copetta chronicles 115

In the cellar   133

Foreword

FROM THE MOMENT I started reading Val Mitchell's delightful introduction to **Polenta on the Board**, I had the sense of rediscovering something precious that was almost lost: a way of living that is familiar, yet increasingly rare. The picture Val paints of her Nonna leaving a tiny town in Italy and arriving in Trail, British Columbia is a story common to my family as well: my husband's grandmother and grandfather also left small towns in Italy to come and settle in the Interior of British Columbia. So, Val's description of "the sisterhood of Italian women" sitting on their front porches in Trail, swapping recipes as they crocheted, was easy for me to imagine.

I felt I was taking part in something worth preserving as I read through (and tasted!) the wonderful recipes and stories of **Polenta on the Board**. There is an underlying theme in this book that time spent preparing food for the family is time well spent. As I made some of the dishes myself, I found I was enjoying the meditation of preparation: the very process of following a longer recipe step by step was somehow a soothing and centering experience. The women making these dishes in the past did not have the luxury of uninterrupted hours they could spend preparing dinner. But they knew how to make meal preparation a priority throughout their day, and lives: they put on the soup to simmer in the morning, and then went out to hoe the garden or scrub the laundry. The process of slow cooking reconnects us to the authentic by reminding us to be attentive to our daily needs.

Given the desire of many of us to slow down and savour life, along with our renewed interest in nutritious homemade food, this book is well-timed. Its emphasis on *la famiglia* (the family) and on delicious gifts of Italian food prepared lovingly and artfully, in a simple kitchen laden with memories, touches a deep, nostalgic chord. It's no surprise that the Slow Food movement, which encourages people worldwide to enjoy leisurely meals of seasonal foods, originated in Italy. Now, the Slow Food movement that began back in 1986 as a reaction to the wide-reaching fast food culture is beginning to catch on here in Canada too. Just in time for **Polenta on the Board**.

When I asked Val why she wrote this book on *la cucina di Nonna* (grandmother's cooking), she admitted that food is her passion, but she is also interested in the role it plays in the fabric of society and family.

Val (who established and for several years operated the Moss Rock Café in Victoria, British Columbia) wanted to let people know that Abruzzese cooking is not difficult, you can do it for very low cost, and it balances good technique and good nutrition. Recording these recipes was also a way for Val to highlight the cuisine of a lesser known region of central Italy. She and her husband Bruce and their daughter Ali had the added delight of "researching" the family recipes by visiting Val's extended family in Antrodoco in the summer of 2002.

Thanks to Val's warm and intimate style, vivid and affectionate descriptions of Nonna's life and foods, and expert presentation of delicious Abruzzese specialties, this book is a treasure. Val's Nonna, Sofia Poscente (Coradetti), epitomizes the Italian matriarch who passed on knowledge, culture, family history, and boundless affection in the kitchen, through the rituals surrounding the careful preparation of food. And according to Val, Nonna's entire family continues to cherish and refine Nonna's recipes even today.

Try, for example, a dish like *involtini di vitello* (veal rolls, which can also be made, as I did, with turkey breast). There are several steps in this recipe, (all quite simple), but the resulting meat rolls, stuffed with *prosciutto*, cheese, and bread crumbs, are so mouth-wateringly good, you will wish you'd made double, believe me.

Or take *stracci*, one of the most unique dishes presented in **Polenta on the Board**. *Stracci* (a meat-filled dinner crepe with tomato sauce) was a favourite dish of Val's late Uncle Ernie Poscente, who was the Vice President of Programming for Shaw Cable at the time that I was hosting and producing the TV show *"Kitchen Culture"* in Duncan, BC.

Ernie, who offered to fly in from Edmonton to prepare *stracci* on the show, was a joy to work with; the *stracci* was a huge hit; and I'm sure you'll agree that this luscious dish is well worth the preparation time. Somehow, knowing that all of Val's family are avid cooks and chefs themselves, carrying on the traditions of Abruzzese cooking in Canada is simply another tribute to the legacy of Nonna's cooking.

Polenta on the Board (which, as you'll learn, is actually slow-cooked coarse cornmeal, covered in a rich sauce and eaten communally) is, as Val points out, a perfect metaphor for the role food plays in her family: a shared experience that brings the family together in a ritual that is essential to our physical and emotional well-being. As an immigrant friend of mine once put it, "Food is love."

That love is warmly evident as you read through, enjoy, prepare, and taste the foods of **Polenta on the Board**. You can feel it as certainly as the sun streaming through Nonna's kitchen windows or the warmth permeating the kitchen from Nonna's wood stove, or from Nonna herself, as she urges you to *"Mangia, Mangia!"* Enjoy!

Star Weiss Fuoco
Author and Editor,
Kitchen Culture, Island Cookery
TV Host, "Kitchen Culture"
Victoria, BC, February, 2003

Ernie Poscente shows Star Weiss Fuoco and her audience how to make stracci.

Photo courtesy
Star Weiss Fuoco

Introduction – "Bechin Povere"

OUR GRANDMOTHER, Nonna Sofia, left school at the age of eight to help care for the younger children in her family in the small town of Antrodoco, Italy. Immigrating to North America at the age of 23 with her husband, two young sons and a daughter (my mother) on the way, Nonna and Papa Poscente settled in the small town of Trail in the mountainous interior of British Columbia, Canada. Papa went off to work at the smelter each day and Nonna cared for my uncles and my mother. Together, they provided for their growing family of five children on Papa's earnings of less than $3 a day by raising, growing and preserving most of their food and relying on Nonna's culinary instincts and inventiveness.

When she left her maternal home in the Abruzzo region of Italy, Nonna brought with her a seasoned knowledge of food—growing it, preserving it and preparing it in the Abruzzese tradition. Nonna's knowledge deepened and her repertoire expanded over the years thanks to a sisterhood of Italian women who would gather in their front porches in the evening and share recipes as they crocheted and embroidered.

When she died in 1985 at the age of 89, the only written recipes Nonna left behind were in a little tattered black book. The contents were a combination of my mother's and my uncles' entries, as dictated by Nonna, as well as a few entries by Nonna in her childlike scrawl and invented spelling. I finally figured out that *"bechin povere"* was not some obscure Italian spice but Nonna's version of "baking powder"!

When I decided to undertake this cookbook project, I eagerly awaited the arrival of the little black book from my mother. This could be the key to the wonderful regional Italian creations which always awaited us in Nonna's kitchen.

I was, unfortunately, wrong. The recipes Nonna had wanted written down were, of course, the ones she was learning from her new, North American home—squares, bars, cookies, birthday cakes—recipes unfamiliar to Nonna but commonplace to us. The recipes I longed for were ones which Nonna did not have to write down because they were part of her being.

Fortunately, through her example, Nonna instilled in her children and grandchildren a love of cooking. She somehow always managed to turn a request for help in the kitchen into an honour. The chance to roll out the *gnocchi* ropes was a rite of passage. Turning the handle on the pasta machine had every bit of status as being the sous-chef in a famous restaurant. Collecting the fresh herbs from the *giardino*, being dispatched to the cellar for a jar of home-preserved *funghi*, peeling the bay leaves off of the sweet *copetta* diamonds for the dessert platter... our apprenticeship was a joyful one.

Nonna knew the value of this gift she gave us. Uncle Julio remembers trying to re-create Nonna's dishes for his own family after he had grown up and moved away from home. Each time he called Nonna for guidance on technique, quantities or ingredients, Nonna would first make him update her on all of the latest news on each of the grandchildren before she would reveal the essential clue to that veal dish or tomato sauce!

Each of us has specialties we learned at Nonna's side and through her guidance over the years. We have expanded Nonna's repertoire through our own experimentation. Many of us have returned to the roots of Nonna's cooking in her native Abruzzo and Antrodoco. We now teach our children and grandchildren the basic techniques and principles Nonna taught us. And for each lesson, there is always a story about growing up in Nonna's kitchen.

It is through these collective experiences and memories of Nonna's children and grandchildren that this cookbook has been created. Nonna would be happy to know you are reading it!

How to use this cookbook

All recipes list the ingredients in the order in which they are used. Since many of the ingredients require preparation (such as chopping, mixing, heating and so on) it is a good idea to start by preparing and assembling all of the ingredients and the required pots, pans and cooking utensils first, before launching in to the recipe.

Fresh pasta dishes which take some time to prepare, such as *stracci, ravioli, lasagna* and *gnocchi*, as well as some sweets, such as *crostoli* and *copetta*, are fun and easier to make with a friend or two. Make large batches so everyone goes home with a dish for their freezer or a platter of sweets.

This type of cooking not only allows experimentation, it embraces it! Feel free to adapt the seasonings to taste, use vegetables on hand instead of those listed for the *minestrone* or fill the *bignè* (cream puffs) with your favourite custard.

Some techniques, such as kneading and rolling fresh pasta, filling the *ravioli* and forming the *gnocchi* improve with practice. If you have an opportunity to make them the first time with someone who has mastered the technique, it is a good way to learn.

Buon appetito!

My sister Lorraine and I help Nonna clean the wild mushrooms.

La Cucina di Nonna – Nonna's Kitchen, Nonna's Cooking

All hallways in Nonna's and Papa's house led to the kitchen. The wonderful, rich aromas drew us like a magnet to the big, bright room which looked through the sun porch out onto the plentiful terraced *giardino*. There was always something bubbling on top of the stove or baking in the old wood oven and Nonna stood ready to satisfy the appetites of whomever entered, no matter the time of day, no matter the number of guests. *"Mangia, mangia!"* encouraged Nonna, as she stood beside us watching as we slurped that first spoonful of delicious *brodo con pastine*. Her satisfaction came from ours; Nonna's cooking was her most loving gift.

Nonna's cooking relied on three things—good quality ingredients, inventive and savoury combinations and practiced techniques. Nonna learned at her Nonna's and mother's sides by watching and doing and she carried that knowledge with her to share with her children and her grandchildren.

Good Italian cooking—*la cucina saporita*—always starts with good ingredients. Two *risotto* dishes, prepared with the same technique and quantities of ingredients, have a completely different taste and consistency if one is made with *arborio* rice and the other with regular long-grain rice.

The range of ingredients in Nonna's cooking was neither large nor exotic. Most fresh produce was grown in the *giardino* or in some cases, such as *stompini* mushrooms and wild dandelion, collected in nearby woods. Most pasta was made *a mano* with fresh farm eggs. Imported cheeses and olive oil were considered staples; Papa would order large forms of *romano* and *pecorino* and *parmigiano* and store them carefully in the cellar cold room, along with the big cans of imported olive oil. Herbs were grown fresh and dried beside the stove or ground together with olive oil into *pesto* and stored in small jars in the cellar pantry.

Feeding a family of seven also required inventiveness. It meant working with ingredients which were available and stretching small amounts of costly ones. Nonna taught us the importance of artfully combining ingredients so that they mutually enhanced each other's good qualities. Some of the combinations were ones Nonna had learned from her early kitchen mentors; others were her own creations. Nonna had an instinctive sense of food which allowed her to know which herbs were called for to enhance the flavour of a sauce or to produce the most savoury stew or soup. She worked with what was on hand, and was constantly expanding the variety of dishes she prepared. No two pots of *minestrone* soup were ever exactly alike!

The third pillar of Nonna's cooking was her practised technique. Whether mixing the *gnocchi* dough, kneading the bread, rolling the pasta or stirring the *polenta*, Nonna worked by sight and feel. We learned never to mix in all of the flour at once when making *gnocchi*, but gradually and just until the dough is *morbido al tatto* (soft to the touch). The size of the eggs and the moisture in the potatoes determine how much flour is needed—a judgment made with each new batch of *gnocchi*. Nonna showed us how often and at what speed to stir the *risotto* so that it achieved just the right creamy-but-*al-dente* consistency. Papa was usually enlisted to stir the big pot of *polenta* as Nonna sprinkled in the coarse cornmeal and watched to make sure that the mixture was bubbling and thickening at just the right pace. Nonna's elusive technique for making *copellu*, the chewy honey-based confection which we eagerly awaited each Christmas season, was legendary.

Nonna picks a fresh fig in her porch

La Cucina Abruzzese – The Cooking of Abruzzo

NONNA WAS BORN Sofia Coradetti on January 22, 1896 in the ancient town of Antrodoco, Italy. Set in a valley in the Appenine range which runs through the centre of Italy, Antrodoco traces its roots back to Roman times when it was an important fortress on the *Via Salaria* ("Salt Road"). The *Via Salaria*, a portion of which still forms part of Italy's highway system, was the main route from Rome to Bari on the Adriatic coast and was used by the Roman Legions to transport salt and other supplies for export to the Eastern Roman Empire.

Antrodoco also sits at the geographic centre of Italy. Although the current official boundaries place Antrodoco on the eastern border of the Lazio region of Italy, the village's roots, traditions and loyalties are in the Abruzzo region. Most Antrodocani are decidedly Abruzzese.

While Antrodoco may be at the centre of the country, the region of Abruzzo is relatively undis-covered compared to its more well-known neighbours of Tuscany, Umbria and Lazio (Rome). Waverly Root, in his classic book **The Food of Italy** was one of the first "outsiders" to shine a light on the cooking of this region, its contributions to the "foodbasket" of Italy and the specialty dishes which are unique to Abruzzese kitchens.

The Abruzzo region has two main cooking traditions, reflecting the geographic duality of the area. Seafood dominates the dishes of the narrow and steep eastern coastal portion, which stretches for 160 kilometres along the Adriatic Sea while lamb, pork, veal, and freshwater fish are central to the cooking of the mountainous interior.

As a result of the relative isolation imposed by the geography, most interior towns have their own local specialties – the *stracci* of Antrodoco, (thin crepes filled with a tomato meat sauce and baked with tomato sauce and cheese), the *scamorza allo spiede* of Rivisondoli, (small mozzarella-type cheese threaded on spits and roasted over hot coals), the *chiodini* of Castelnuovo, (long-stemmed wild mushrooms which grow among poplar tree stumps), and the *fagioli bianchi* of Capestrano (a specialty white bean served in a tomato sauce over pasta), to name a few. The town of L'Aquila is renowned for the tradition of the *panarda*, a spectacular two-day banquet of at least thirty courses, held to celebrate a significant event in a family or the community.

Cornmeal is a staple in Abruzzese kitchens. While it is used in a number of baked goods, the most well known Italian cornmeal-based dish is *polenta*. *Polenta* is slow-cooked coarse cornmeal usually served with a tomato-based meat sauce or cut into wedges and grilled in olive oil. The Abruzzese tradition is to serve the *polenta* on a board (*polenta sulla tavola*), with each diner pulling up a chair, taking up their fork and eating right off of the board.

Pasta, a mainstay in the Abruzzese diet, is often made fresh in one's home and cut into the familiar shapes of *spaghetti, tagliatelle, lasagne, fettucine, linguine, vermicelli* and, for soups, small *pastine*. *Cicerciole*, tiny squares cut from fresh *fettucine* strands, are a favourite local *pastina*. *Maccheroni alla chitarra* (guitar pasta), a specialty of the area, is so-named because of the wooden frame with strings fastened tautly across it used to cut the dough into strips. The signature pasta of Antrodoco is the cylindrical *ciufulitti* (similar to the more commonly recognized *bucatini*). *Gnocchi* (tiny potato, egg and flour dumplings, tossed in a tomato or meat sauce) is a favourite in any Italian home. The hand-rolled morsels bear little resemblance to the mass-produced version which has made its way to North American grocery shelves in recent years.

Cheese is used liberally in Abruzzese kitchens, a favourite being *pecorino*, made from the milk of sheep which graze in the mountain pastures in the region. (The Italian word for sheep is *pecora*.) The mild, delicate taste of fresh, tender *pecorino* is delicious on its own. Aged, the sharp, salty flavour of *pecorino* brings pasta or soups alive and is a satisfying counterpoint to fresh pear, peach, or figs for a simple dessert. *Ricotta*, a soft, white, unsalted cheese, also made from sheep's milk, is used extensively as well, simply sliced onto bread and eaten with fresh tomatoes and a generous grinding of pepper and salt or used in soups, pasta dishes, or desserts. *Scamorza*, sometimes compared to the water buffalo mozzarella of Campania but made from cow's milk in Abruzzo, is a good melting cheese for dishes like *frittata* (omelette) or baked pasta dishes.

The mountainous terrain in the Abruzzo interior makes gardening challenging, but most homes have their hillside terraced *giardino* which supplies the fresh **vegetables and herbs** for drying, preserving or using fresh in the many soup and vegetable dishes in Abruzzese cooking. Roma tomatoes, zucchini, sweet peppers, hot peppers, onions, artichokes, beets, asparagus, spinach, *radicchio*, chick peas, fava beans, green peas, and string beans share the terraced beds with the staple herbs of basil, rosemary, dill, thyme, oregano, and bay. The mountain slopes complement this cultivated bounty with wild herbs and flowers such as thyme, oregano, poppies and crocus (saffron), while the forests are home to wild dandelion and mushrooms. Groves of chestnut trees produce the edible *castagne* (chestnuts) which are roasted and eaten after a winter meal or cooked and made into a paste for use in baking.

The ancient town of Antrodoco sits at the geographic centre of Italy.

ITALY

Antrodoco

ABRUZZO

SARDINIA

SICILY

Seasonal Rhythms

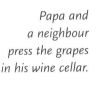

THERE WAS ALWAYS A CONNECTION between what was going on inside Nonna's kitchen and what was going on outside. When the *giardino* (garden) was producing, from late spring to early autumn, Nonna's kitchen was always a flurry of preserving, while on the stove bubbled a soup of fresh vegetables for that night's first course. When the dandelion leaves were just the right colour of green with that perfect silky texture, a dandelion salad was the grand finale of our meal. When the raspberries were plump and delicious, a bowl of them, picked in our pyjamas, sprinkled with a touch of sugar and drizzled with milk was breakfast for the lucky grandchild who had a sleepover at Nonna's the night before. A favourite and simple summer dessert paired the freshness of juicy peach slices and the maturity of homemade red wine, prepared right at the table after a summer meal.

Growing up in Antrodoco, Nonna learned as a young girl that nourishing a family meant being both prepared and inventive. There were no corner stores to run to for a dozen eggs, no freezers full of frozen meat and vegetables, no local supermarkets with everything from fresh herbs in the dead of winter to a dizzying array of meats, seafoods, sauces and dairy products. In this ancient town in the mountains of central Italy, a meal was built from the ingredients and preserves which were always kept in sufficient supply, supplemented by those which were freshly available at that moment.

Even though the modern conveniences of supermarkets, freezers and fast food eventually surrounded Nonna in her adopted North American home, the rhythms of Nonna's kitchen were those which sustained her as a child.

Nonna and Papa created a self-sufficient world in the modest house in which they settled and raised their family. The shelves in the basement root cellar had empty jars of various sizes ready to be filled and preserved with the harvest from the terraced *giardino*, or the wild *funghi* gathered from their secret forest locations in the area, for use over the cold winter months. Deep red plum tomatoes were laid out to dry on netting in the enclosed front sunporch next to the big, potted fig tree drooping with its purple tear-shaped fruit. The sun-dried tomatoes added a rich flavour to Nonna's sauces throughout the year. The pantry close to the kitchen housed tall canisters of flour, sugar, cornmeal and dried goods, within easy reach for baking that day's bread or making pasta, *polenta* or *gnocchi* for dinner.

Papa and a neighbour press the grapes in his wine cellar.

The Soup Pot

"La cena e pronta!" Our call to the dinner table meant that the traditional first course— a steaming bowl of homemade soup—awaited us. After we gave thanks, a bowl of freshly grated *romano* or *parmigiano* cheese and a basket of thick slices of homemade bread made their way around the table and our meal officially began.

A meal without soup was rare in Nonna's kitchen. Whether it was a simple *brodo con pastine* or a heartier *minestrone*, a pot of *zuppa* was always ready on Nonna's stovetop.

Most soups started with a homemade chicken or beef broth. The delicate, comforting taste of the broth was created by using two different cuts of meat and a variety of mild tasting vegetables and letting everything simmer for several hours to allow the flavours to mingle.

The ingredients depended on the season and what was available in Nonna's pantry. When the *giardino* was producing, Nonna would create a summer *minestrone*, a zucchini soup or a rice soup with asparagus or fresh spinach or baby peas. Winter soups typically used dried beans or *ceci*, preserved tomatoes, root vegetables and winter greens such as cabbage and *radicchio*. At any time of the year, a clear broth with *pastine* or a *stracciatella* provided a lighter first course.

Kai Poscente enjoys some brodo while cousin Val looks on.

Soup
recipes

Basic chicken broth

Makes approximately 12 cups (3 litres)

*This broth is the base for numerous soups and sauces
so it's a good idea to make a large pot and keep some on hand in the freezer.
(I also freeze some in ice-cube trays for recipes which require only small quantities.)*

12 cups (3 l) cold water (approximately)

one 2–3 lb. (1–1.5 kg) stewing hen,
quartered or the equivalent weight
of chicken backs and necks

one 1 lb. (500 g) beef bone
(neck bone is best)

4 large carrots, washed and peeled

4 stalks celery (including the leaves),
washed and trimmed

1 large onion, peeled

1 small tomato

several sprigs of fresh parsley

salt and freshly ground pepper

Fill a large stock pot half full with cold water and add the cut up stewing hen and the beef bone to the pot. Bring everything to a gentle boil and let it cook for 15 minutes, skimming off and discarding the foam as it accumulates on the surface.

Cut up the vegetables roughly, add them to the pot and bring everything back to a boil. Add the parsley and salt and pepper to taste, reduce the heat and let it simmer slowly, covered for 2–3 hours, stirring occasionally.

Taste it and adjust for salt and pepper. Pour the soup through a colander placed over a large bowl and strain out the meat, bones and vegetables. Reserve the cooked chicken meat for other purposes and discard the remaining bones and vegetables *or*, if you wish to add a little body and colour to the broth, mash a few of the carrots finely and add them back into the broth.

Cool the broth thoroughly, then refrigerate it for a few hours until the fat solidifies on the surface and can be easily removed. Skim off and discard the fat, reheat the broth and strain it a second time. Allow it to cool.

Store the chicken broth in an air-tight container in the fridge for up to one week or freeze it. Use the broth in recipes for soups, sauces, vegetables, pastas or *risotto*.

Basic beef broth

makes approximately 12 cups (3 litres)

*This broth has a more intense flavour than chicken broth
when used in sauces, risotto and soups.*

12 cups (3 l) cold water (approximately)
one 2 lb. (1 kg) beef shank
one 2 lb. (1 kg) beef brisket
4 large carrots, washed and peeled
4 stalks celery (including leaves),
washed and trimmed
1 large onion, outer brown peels
removed but inner brown peel
left intact
2 small tomatoes, washed
1 small potato, peeled
1 Tbsp. (15 ml) *pesto* **or** 2 tsp. (10 ml)
dried Italian herbs
salt and freshly ground pepper

Fill a large stock pot half full with cold water and add the shank and brisket
to the pot. Bring the water to a gentle boil and cook for 15 minutes,
skimming off and discarding the foam as it accumulates on the surface.

Cut up the vegetables roughly, add them to the pot, and bring everything
back to a boil. (Leave the inner layers of peel on the onion to deepen the
colour of the broth.) Add the *pesto*, add salt and pepper to taste, reduce the
heat and let it simmer, covered, for 2–3 hours.

Taste it and adjust for salt and pepper. Using a colander over a large bowl,
strain out and discard the meat, bones and vegetables.

Cool the broth thoroughly, then refrigerate it for a few hours until the fat
solidifies on the surface and can be easily removed. Skim off and discard the
fat, reheat the broth and strain it a second time. Allow it to cool.

Store the broth in an air-tight container in the fridge for up to 1 week or in
the freezer. Use it in soup, *risotto* and sauce recipes.

Easy fish stock

makes 6 cups

This is an easy to prepare fish stock to use in risotto or soups.

1 1/2 lb. (750 g) of any fish scraps
(heads, bones, tails), except salmon
7 cups (1.8 l) water
1 onion, chopped
2 celery stalks, chopped
2 bay leaves
1 tsp. (5 ml) fennel seeds
1 tsp. (5 ml) peppercorns

In a large pot, mix together all the ingredients, bring the mixture just to a boil, then reduce the heat and simmer, uncovered, for 20 minutes.

Strain the stock through a fine sieve. Use it immediately or freeze it for future use.

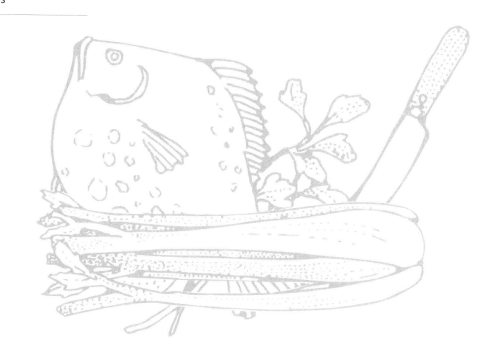

Brodo con cicerciole

BROTH WITH TINY PASTA SQUARES

serves 4–6

When Nonna made fresh pasta, she usually cut some of it into "cicerciole" – fettucine noodles cut into little squares.
Any of the wide variety of packaged "pastine" (little pasta) can also be used in this simple, delicate soup
which provides immediate comfort with the first satisfying spoonful.
A wonderful light start to a meal, this broth is also reputed to have curative powers for winter colds or flu!

8 cups (2 l) chicken broth

1/2 cup (125 ml) *cicerciole* or *pastine*
(*acini di pepe, stelle*)

grated *parmigiano* or *romano* cheese

salt and freshly ground pepper

Bring the broth to a boil in a medium saucepan.

Add the *cicerciole* or *pastine* to the boiling broth and stir a few times to prevent them from clumping.

Cook the soup at a gentle boil until the *pastine* are just *al dente*, taste and adjust for salt and pepper, then ladle the soup into individual bowls and sprinkle it with grated cheese. Pass around extra grated cheese.

Note: Pasta will continue to expand and get unpleasantly soft in leftover soup. To prevent this, strain the leftover soup and store the strained *pastine* in a separate bowl so that they do not continue to absorb fluid. To reheat, heat the broth first and add the reserved *pastine* to the hot broth just before serving.

Stracciatella

ITALIAN EGG-DROP SOUP

serves 6

*Straccio means rag, a description of the egg and cheese mixture
which cooks almost upon contact with the hot broth in this classic Italian soup.
Lightly steamed spinach is sometimes added to create a heartier dish.*

8 cups (2 l) chicken or beef broth
3 large eggs
3 Tbsp. (45 ml) grated *romano* or
   parmigiano cheese
3 Tbsp. (45 ml) flour
grated *romano* or *parmigiano* cheese
salt and freshly ground pepper
chopped fresh Italian parsley for garnish

Whisk the eggs in a medium bowl with a pourable spout, then add the cheese and whisk well, then add the flour very gradually and whisk the mixture until it is smooth. Set it aside.

Bring the broth to a gentle boil in a medium saucepan. Just before you are ready to serve the soup, drizzle the egg-cheese mixture into the simmering broth while stirring slowly and steadily with a wooden spoon. Stir and simmer for 1 minute, just until the egg mixture resembles little rags (*stracciatelle*).

Serve the soup immediately with a sprinkle of grated cheese, fresh parsley garnish and salt and pepper to taste.

Zuppa di verdure e riso
SOUP WITH GREENS AND RICE

serves 6

*A satisfying and healthy soup
when the garden greens are growing in profusion!*

1 cup (250 ml) water, lightly salted

4 cups (1 l) of either fresh spinach leaves, beet greens, dandelion, Swiss chard, or radicchio, washed and stems removed

1 small onion, chopped finely

2 Tbsp. (30 ml) butter

6 cups (1.5 l) beef broth

1/3 cup (125 g) uncooked short grain rice

freshly ground pepper

grated *romano* cheese

Bring the salted water to a boil in a pot large enough to hold the spinach (or other greens). Add the greens to the boiling water, cover and let it cook for 3–4 minutes or just until the greens are wilted.

Put a strainer over a bowl and drain the greens through the strainer, reserving the cooking liquid. Lay the drained greens out on a cutting board and roughly chop them.

Sauté the butter and onions together in a medium pan for 6–8 minutes at medium heat until the onion is translucent and golden. Add the drained, cooked greens to the onion-butter mixture, stir to combine and sauté the mixture at medium-high for 2–3 minutes.

Place the broth, the onion-and-greens mixture and the rice in a pot, add the reserved cooking liquid from the greens, stir once and bring everything to a gentle boil. Cover and cook the soup at medium heat for 15 minutes or just until the rice is cooked.

Serve the soup immediately with a grinding of black pepper and a generous sprinkle of *romano* cheese.

Zuppa di ricotta e pasta
RICOTTA AND PASTA SOUP

serves 6

My sister Lorraine and I each remember Nonna making this quick soup for us with a different pasta.
Lorraine's favourite was the small bucatini tubes; mine was Nonna's homemade tagliatelle.
Either way, the result is subtle, creamy and satisfying, especially with a generous sprinkle of romano cheese and lots of parsley.

This soup is best with Italian ricotta which is made from sheep's milk and has a richer taste and firmer texture
than some other varieties. If using the latter, you will need to add more salt and cheese to give the soup taste
(and don't try to substitute cottage cheese!).

1/2 cup (125 ml) *bucatini* pasta,
    broken into 1" (2.5 cm) pieces

1 Tbsp. (15 ml) butter

1 cup (250 ml) *ricotta*

6 cups (1.5 l) chicken broth, heated
    to a gentle boil

salt and freshly ground pepper

fresh Italian parsley, chopped

grated *romano* cheese

Bring a medium saucepan of salted water to a boil. Add the pasta and cook until the pasta is *al dente* (approximately 8 minutes).

Drain and place the pasta back in the pot. Stir in the butter and *ricotta*.

Pour in the heated chicken broth, stir and let the soup simmer for another minute, just long enough to heat the *ricotta* through.

Remove from the heat and serve it immediately, garnished with a generous sprinkling of *romano* cheese, a good grinding of black pepper and some fresh parsley.

Minestra di pasta e fagioli
PASTA AND BEAN SOUP

serves 8–10

This hearty soup is a meal in itself. Cannelini beans are white and smaller than kidney beans and have a thinner skin. They are available in most Italian markets, dried or canned. If not available, white navy beans work well, too. For a vegetarian version, use a vegetable broth.

1 cup (250 ml) dried *cannellini* beans **or** one 19-oz. (540 ml) jar of cooked beans, drained

4 cups (1 l) beef or vegetable broth

6–8 cups (1.5–2 l) water

1 large carrot, peeled and cut in large chunks

1 celery stalk, thinly sliced

1 large potato, halved

3 Tbsp. (45 ml) extra virgin olive oil

1 onion, finely chopped

1 garlic clove, minced

3 Tbsp. (45 ml) chopped Italian parsley **or** 1 Tbsp. (15 ml) *pesto*

3 large tomatoes, peeled, seeded and roughly chopped **or** one 28 oz. (796 ml) tin of tomatoes, drained, seeds removed and pulp roughly chopped

salt and freshly ground pepper

1 cup (250 ml) elbow macaroni or small shell pasta

grated *parmigiano* cheese

If using dried beans, soak the beans in cold water overnight, then drain and rinse them thoroughly.

In a large soup pot, add the broth, water, carrot, celery, potato and soaked beans. (If you are using canned beans, do not add them yet.) Cover and bring everything to a boil. Reduce the heat and simmer the mixture for 1 hour, stirring occasionally.

While the beans and vegetables are cooking, heat the oil in a pan and sauté the onion and garlic for 6–8 minutes or until they are translucent and golden. Add the parsley, stir in the tomato pulp, season with salt and pepper, and simmer this mixture, uncovered, for 20 minutes.

With a slotted spoon, remove the potato and carrot pieces, and 1 cup (250 ml) of the beans-and-celery mixture from the soup pot, put them in a bowl and mash them. If you are using canned beans, mash one cup (250 ml) of them with the vegetables and add the rest of them, unmashed, to the soup pot.

Return the mashed vegetable and bean mixture to the soup pot, add the tomato-onion mixture to the pot and bring everything to a gentle simmer for 25–30 minutes.

Just before serving, bring the soup to a boil, add the pasta and cook, uncovered, for a further 10 minutes or just until the pasta is *al dente*. Taste the soup and adjust for salt and pepper. Serve it immediately with *parmigiano* cheese.

Minestrone d'estate

SOUP OF SUMMER VEGETABLES

serves 6–8

Nonna created a summer minestrone *with whatever vegetables were being harvested in the* giardino.
No two pots were ever exactly the same but each of them was memorable!

2 Tbsp. (30 ml) extra virgin olive oil

2 Tbsp. (30 ml) butter

1 garlic clove, crushed and minced

1 large onion, chopped

2 large tomatoes, peeled*, seeded
and chopped

6–8 cups (1.5–2 l) water

2 celery stalks, thinly sliced

3 large carrots, peeled and sliced

6 small potatoes, peeled and cut into
bite-sized pieces

1/2 lb. (250 g) green beans, sliced into
1" (2.5 cm) lengths

1 cup (250 ml) fresh shelled peas, **or**
1 cup (250 ml) frozen peas, unthawed

1/2 lb. (250 g) beet greens or Swiss chard,
stems removed and leaves torn

1 small zucchini, scrubbed well, halved
lengthwise and sliced into 1/4"
(6 mm) slices

handful of fresh Italian parsley and basil,
mixed and chopped

salt and freshly ground pepper

freshly grated *parmigiano* cheese

In a large soup pot, heat the oil, butter, garlic and onions and sauté for 6–8 minutes until the onions are translucent and golden.

Add the tomatoes, sauté for another 10 minutes, then add 6 cups (1.5 l) of water, and all of the remaining vegetables and herbs. Salt and pepper to taste, then let the *minestrone* simmer for an hour, stirring it occasionally and adding more water if it gets too thick.

Serve the minestrone with *parmigiano* cheese.

* *Note*: To peel fresh tomatoes, plunge them in a pot of boiling water for approximately 30–40 seconds, remove them from the water with a slotted spoon and pierce the skin with a sharp knife. The skin should peel off easily.

Minestrone d'inverno

SOUP OF WINTER VEGETABLES

serves 8–10

This soup uses preserved and root vegetables. Nonna used dried beans but it can be made with canned beans as well.
Add the drained canned beans late in the cooking process so they retain their shape and texture.

1 cup (250 ml) dried *cannelini* beans **or** one 19 oz. (540 ml) jar, drained

2 Tbsp. (30 ml) oil

2 Tbsp. (30 ml) butter

1 large onion, chopped

1 garlic clove, minced

one 28 oz. (796 ml) can tomatoes, seeded and chopped roughly

6–8 cups (1–1.5 l) water

2 large potatoes, peeled and cut into bite-sized pieces

2 large carrots, peeled and sliced

2 cups (500 ml) roughly chopped cabbage

1 Tbsp. (15 ml) *pesto di verdure* **or** 2 tsp. (10 ml) dried Italian seasoning

salt and freshly ground pepper

1 cup (250 ml) *conchigliette* pasta

grated *romano* or *parmigiano* cheese

If you are using dried beans, soak them overnight in cold water, then rinse and drain them well. Discard the soaking liquid.

In a large soup pot, heat the oil, butter, garlic and onions and sauté for 6–8 minutes until the onions are translucent and golden. Add the tomatoes, and sauté for a further 10 minutes.

Add the water, the soaked beans and all of the vegetables and *pesto*. If you are using canned beans, do not add them at this point. Add salt and pepper to taste and simmer the soup for one hour or longer.

Increase the heat and add the pasta (and the canned beans, if using) when the soup is bubbling. Cook for a further 7 or 8 minutes or until the pasta is *al dente*. Serve the *minestrone* hot with grated cheese.

Zuppa di lenticchie di Zio Giulio
UNCLE JULIO'S LENTIL SOUP

serves 4

*Uncle Julio saves the rind from parmigiano cheese to add to hearty soups and sauces as they simmer.
It enhances the flavour in a subtle but distinctively rustic way.*

Uncle Julio made a big pot of his lentil soup in our café one day and there wasn't a drop left.

2 Tbsp. (30 ml) finely chopped
yellow onion

4 Tbsp. (60 ml) extra virgin olive oil

3 Tbsp. (45 ml) butter

2 Tbsp. (30 ml) each finely chopped
celery and carrots

1/8 lb. (60 g) *prosciutto*, diced or
shredded

1 cup (250 ml) canned plum tomatoes,
seeded and roughly chopped

1/2 lb. (250 g) brown lentils, rinsed and
drained

5 cups (1.2 l) beef broth

2 cups (500 ml) water

salt & freshly ground pepper

rind of *parmigiano* cheese (if available)

4 Tbsp. (60 ml) *parmigiano* cheese

In a large pot, sauté the onions in the oil and butter at medium heat for 8–10 minutes or until they are soft and lightly golden.

Add the celery and carrot and simmer for 3–4 minutes, stirring regularly to prevent burning. Add the *prosciutto* and sauté for another minute.

Add the chopped tomatoes and their juice and simmer for 30 minutes, stirring from time to time. Add the rinsed and drained lentils and stir to distribute evenly.

Stir in 4 cups (1 l) of broth (reserving one cup) and the water, add 6 or 7 grindings of pepper, salt to taste (the *prosciutto* adds saltiness so be careful not to oversalt) and the *parmigiano* rind (if available).

Simmer slowly for 50–60 minutes, checking it after 40 minutes and adding more broth if the soup is too thick. At the end of the cooking process, remove and discard the *parmigiano* rind before serving. Pass the grated cheese.

Polenta on the board

ONE OF THE MAIN pieces of equipment in Nonna's kitchen was a huge board which Papa made for her in his basement workshop. Nonna kept it meticulously cleaned and carefully oiled and, over time, the board deepened to a rich golden colour and always carried the scent of warm, fresh-baked bread.

The work surface of the board was used for making *gnocchi*, laying out the fresh pasta strips, kneading the bread dough—and eating *polenta* the Abruzzese way!

On *polenta* nights, the board was placed on top of the dining table and the thick, steaming cornmeal was spread out across the board, topped with a long-simmered tomato sauce with sausages or spareribs or meatballs and finished with a generous sprinkle of freshly grated *parmigiano* or *romano* cheese. "Setting the table" involved providing everyone with a fork, for *Polenta sulla Tavola* (Polenta on the Board) means just that—pulling up a chair, taking your fork in hand and digging in!

What a delight that was to be a child at a *polenta* meal. This great edible canvas stretched out in front of us, waiting for our designs to start with our first forkful and then the next and the next after that. All around the table, grown-ups and kids were creating their own road systems through our shared *polenta* town. It never occurred to us that this might seem odd to people who didn't share the same tradition— like Uncle Julio's childhood friend who dropped by at dinnertime and fell speechless as he stared at the family gathered around the kitchen table which was covered in a *polenta* on the board. Nonna didn't skip a beat. She got up, pulled another chair up to the table, handed him a fork and commanded, *"Siedeti! Mangia!"* He dutifully sat down, followed Uncle Julio's lead and within minutes was enthusiastically forging his own road into the *polenta*.

Cooking the *polenta* usually involved two sets of hands – one to stir the big pot of water heating up on the stove while the other poured in the cornmeal in a thin stream. The pouring and stirring were carefully synchronized to prevent lumps. As the cornmeal started to thicken, Papa usually took over the stirring with the strong, long-handled wooden spoon, singing the song, *"Polenta mia polenta, Tu fume e io sto qui, Se entro in grazia di Papa, Ti faccio fumo io!"* (Loosely translated: "Polenta my polenta, you're steaming away and I'm here waiting. If I'm blessed, I'll eat you right up!")

When the *polenta* was ready, Papa would lift the big steaming pot from the stove and carry it to the table where the board lay waiting. As he poured it into the centre of the board, Nonna spread it with the back of the big wooden spoon until it reached almost to each edge in a consistent thickness. After letting the *polenta* set for a minute or two, Papa held the big pot of tomato meat sauce which had been simmering for a few hours on the stove while Nonna used a ladle to deposit steaming puddles of sauce in a polka-dot pattern across the corn-yellow base. There were always young volunteers eager to take over from there to carefully distribute the puddles until all of the dots joined together to form a solid layer of sauce, ready to receive the freshly grated cheese which Nonna sprinkled over all of it.

At the end of the meal, when we had no room for more, Nonna carefully cut around our network of trails and stored the untouched *polenta* away to be baked and served for next day's lunch — an encore as delicious as the main event!

The tradition of *polenta sulla tavola* originated in the Abruzzo region of Italy and many families continue the tradition in their North American homes. Debates over the ideal cooking process — the temperature the water should be when the *polenta* is added, how long the *polenta* needs to be stirred, how long it needs to cook — can become heated, and rarely are firmly-held opinions altered. The debate, like Papa's song, is all part of the tradition of *polenta* on the board!

Uncle Julio sprinkles the cheese as Nonna ladles on the sauce.

Polenta, pasta, sauce and risotto recipes

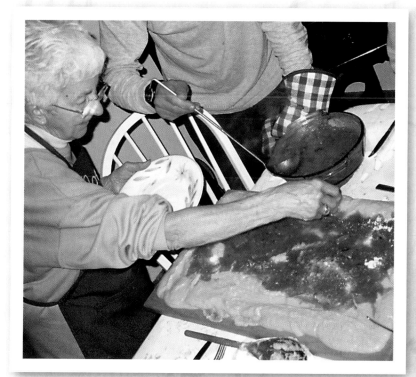

LEFT: *Nonna's children have carried on the tradition of* polenta *on the board.*

Nonna used a board which covered most of the table. My mother Eleanor now uses a smaller board to accomodate a smaller crowd.

(See Polenta on the board *recipe, page 27.)*

RIGHT: *Nonna's great-grandson Harley Sovran scoops the first of several helpings of* polenta *at a family gathering.*

With a larger board, the polenta *is eaten right off the board.*

(See Polenta story, *page 24.)*

Pork is used extensively in preserved products such as
sausage and prosciutto (cured ham) in Abruzzo.

Homemade pork sausages, like these prepared by Pietro Pascasi
in his Antrodoco home, are delicious grilled or long-simmered
in a tomato sauce and served on top of polenta.

(See Polenta con salsicce on page 30.)

Polenta on the board

serves 6–8 people (for a smaller crowd, see note on page 28)

You will need a large heavy pot and a strong wooden spoon with a handle long enough to comfortably stir the polenta *in the pot and to avoid getting burned by popping bubbles. Make sure that the cornmeal is coarsely ground, not the finer ground variety which is used in baking or for cooked cereal. If you don't have a board, simply make individual servings by spreading the* polenta *on each person's plate and topping with the sauce and grated cheese.*

16–18 cups (4–4.5 l) cold water

2 tsp. (10 ml) salt

4 1/2 cups (1.1 l) coarse ground
    cornmeal

2 tsp. (10 ml) butter

sauce for 6–8 (see over for
    suggestions)

2 cups (500 ml) freshly grated
    parmigiano or *romano* cheese

My mother, Eleanor, stirs and watches intently as the polenta *thickens.*

Place the clean oiled board on top of your serving table.

Put 16 cups (4 l) of the water and the salt in a large heavy pot and place it on a large element on the stovetop. Put the cornmeal in an easy-pour container and drizzle the cornmeal into the water, stirring gently and constantly with a wooden spoon to prevent lumps from forming. Press any lumps that do form against the side of the pot to disperse the cornmeal.

Turn the heat to high and continue stirring after all of the cornmeal has been added. When the mixture starts to boil, adjust the temperature so that a steady gentle bubbling is maintained.

Continue stirring and cooking for 30–35 minutes or until the mixture is thick enough for the spoon to stand up in it for 3 or 4 seconds

Continued on next page

Adding the
final touches

and the cornmeal grains lose their grittiness. If it gets too thick too early in the cooking process, add a little more water. The cooking time will vary depending on the type of pot used. A lighter pot requires a longer cooking time since you will have to keep the temperature lower to prevent burning.

Stir in the butter, remove the pot from the stove and pour the cooked *polenta* into the centre of the board. Immediately spread the hot *polenta* over the board with the wet wooden spoon or spatula, to a consistent thickness of approximately 1" (2.5 cm). (If you are not using a board, ladle the *polenta* onto each person's plate and spread it into a layer.)

Let the *polenta* sit for a few minutes to set, then ladle the sauce at regular intervals on top of the *polenta*. Gently disperse the sauce so that it forms a smooth layer over the *polenta*. Finish with a generous sprinkling of freshly grated cheese. Provide everyone with a fork and a big napkin!

After people have finished eating, cut out any remaining untouched *polenta* and place it in a casserole dish, to be baked just until hot the next day for lunch.

Note: **For a smaller crowd**, the recipe can be halved. Allow approximately 3 1/2 cups (875 ml) of water to one cup (250 ml) of cornmeal and reduce the butter and salt proportionately.

Sauces for Polenta on the Board:
Polenta can be topped with *Polenta con costicine di maiale* (page 29) or *Polenta con salsicce* (page 30) or with your choice of *ragu* or *sugo*.

Polenta con costicine di maiale

POLENTA WITH PORK SPARERIBS

serves 6–8

This is a rich, succulent sauce which pairs perfectly with the relatively mild taste of the polenta.
The spareribs are meant to be eaten with your fingers so have a good supply of napkins ready!

1/4 cup safflower or vegetable oil

5 lb. (2.5 kg) pork spareribs, cut into single ribs

4 Tbsp. (60 ml) extra virgin olive oil

one medium onion, finely chopped

2 garlic cloves, pressed and finely chopped

three 28 oz. (796 ml) tins plum tomatoes, seeded and chopped

one 5.5 oz. (156 ml) tin tomato paste, mixed with 1/2 cup (125 ml) chicken or beef broth

one large carrot, peeled and finely minced or finely grated

2 bay leaves

1 tsp. (5 ml) marjoram

2 or 3 fresh sage leaves **or** 1/2 tsp. (2 ml) dried sage

1 pinch of hot chilli pepper flakes (opt.)

salt and freshly ground pepper

polenta for 6–8 people (See page 27)

2 cups (500 ml) freshly grated *parmigiano* or *romano* cheese

Heat the vegetable oil to medium high in a large heavy sauté pan. Brown the ribs on both sides. (If the pan is not large enough to hold the ribs in one layer, brown them in stages.) Remove the browned ribs to a platter and keep them warm.

In a pot large enough to eventually hold all of the ingredients, heat the olive oil and the onions and sauté for 6–8 minutes or until they are translucent. Add the garlic and sauté for a further 3–4 minutes.

Add the tomatoes, tomato paste and broth mixture, minced carrot, herbs, hot chilli flakes (if using), salt and pepper to taste. Cook this mixture for half an hour at medium heat, stirring it occasionally and breaking up any large pieces of tomato.

Taste it and adjust for salt and pepper, then add the browned spareribs and simmer everything together for at least two hours, stirring periodically.

Half an hour before you are ready to eat, cook the *polenta* as on page 27.

Spread the cooked *polenta* on the prepared board. Spoon the liquid part of the sauce on top of the *polenta* and gently spread it to distribute. Then distribute the spareribs around the *polenta* and finish with a generous sprinkling of *parmigiano* or *romano* cheese.

Polenta con salsicce

POLENTA WITH ITALIAN SAUSAGES

serves 8

5 Tbsp. (60 ml) extra virgin olive oil

3 lbs. (1.5 kg) good quality Italian sausage (hot or regular, depending on your preference), cut into 2" (5 cm) pieces

1 lb. (500 g) lean ground beef or veal

one large onion, minced

two garlic cloves, crushed and minced

three 28 oz. (796 ml) tins plum tomatoes, seeded and roughly chopped

one 5.5 oz. (156 ml) tin tomato paste, mixed with 1/2 cup (125 ml) chicken or beef stock

one large carrot, peeled and finely minced or finely grated

2 Tbsp. (30 ml) *pesto di verdure* **or** 1 tsp. (5 ml) **each** dried oregano, thyme, basil and rosemary

salt and freshly ground pepper

polenta for 6–8 people (See page 27)

2 cups (500 ml) freshly grated *parmigiano* or *romano* cheese

In a sauté pan, heat 3 Tbsp. (45 ml) of the olive oil in a large pot and brown the sausage pieces on all sides. Remove the sausage pieces with a slotted spoon and set them aside.

In the same pan, sauté the ground beef or veal until all pink disappears. Remove the ground meat from the pan with a slotted spoon and reserve it with the sausages.

In a pot large enough to eventually hold all of the ingredients, heat the remaining 2 Tbsp. (30 ml) of olive oil and the onions and sauté for 6–8 minutes or until the onions are translucent. Add the garlic and sauté for a further 3–4 minutes.

Add the tomatoes, tomato paste-broth mixture, the minced carrot, *pesto* or herbs, a generous pinch of salt and several grindings of fresh pepper. Simmer this mixture for 1/2 hour, then add the reserved sausages and ground beef and simmer for two more hours, stirring periodically and tasting to adjust for salt and pepper after an hour of cooking.

Half an hour before you are ready to eat, cook the *polenta* as on page 27.

Spread the cooked *polenta* on the prepared board. Spoon the sauce over the *polenta*, distributing the sausage pieces within easy reach of all diners. Finish with a generous sprinkling of *parmigiano* or *romano* cheese.

Polenta crostini misti

MIXED POLENTA CANAPES

makes forty 2" (5 cm) squares

In addition to serving polenta *on the board, there are numerous ways to "dress" and serve* polenta.
As well as being delicious, polenta *provides a versatile wheat-free alternative to pasta and bread.
For example, cooked* polenta *can be spread out in a thin layer on a cookie pan, left to cool and then sliced into croutons
for salads or sliced into squares, grilled and topped with your favourite ingredients and served as finger food, an* antipasto
or a light lunch. Ingredients such as diced roasted red peppers or sautéed garlic can be added toward the end of the polenta
cooking process to produce a colourful confetti effect in the bright yellow cornmeal and add flavour to the mild cornmeal taste.

7–8 cups (1.8–2 l) cold water

2 tsp. (10 ml) salt

2 cups (500 ml) coarsely ground cornmeal

1 tsp. (5 ml) butter

1/2 cup (125 ml) grated *parmigiano* cheese

freshly ground pepper

2 Tbsp. (30 ml) butter, melted

Suggestions for garnish:

4 oz. (125 g) *gorgonzola* or *cambozola*
cheese, sliced into 20 small slices

20 thin 2" (5 cm) long strips of roasted
red peppers

20 peeled garlic cloves from 2 heads of
roasted garlic (see below)

1/2 cup (125 ml) *pesto di basilico* or your
favourite *pesto*

1 cup (250 ml) grated *asiago* or *fontina*
cheese

1/3 cup (80 ml) pine nuts, lightly toasted

Cook the *polenta* cornmeal using method described on page 27, but in a smaller pot. (It may cook a bit faster, 25–30 minutes). At the end of the cooking process, stir in the butter and the *parmigiano* cheese just before removing the *polenta* from the heat.

Instead of pouring the cooked *polenta* onto a board, pour it onto a lightly greased 11" x 17" (28 x 42 cm) cookie pan and spread it evenly to the edges, using a spatula dipped in water. (For a thicker *polenta* layer, use a 10" x 14" (25 x 36 cm) buttered pan or casserole dish.) Let it cool to set. (This can be made ahead and kept covered in the fridge for several hours or overnight.)

Just before you are ready to serve, place a rack at the highest level in your oven and turn on the broiler.

Cut the cooled *polenta* into 2" (5 cm) squares, brush both sides lightly with the melted butter and grind a light dusting of pepper over them. Arrange the squares on two cookie pans so there is space between the squares.

Place the pans under a hot broiler and broil the *polenta* squares on the top rack for 4 or 5 minutes, turn them over and broil the other side for a further

Continued on next page

4 or 5 minutes or until the edges are golden and lightly crusty. Remove the squares from the oven.

Garnish the tops of half of the squares with 1 tsp. (5 ml) of *pesto* (spread to distribute), a pinch of grated *asiago* or *fontina* cheese and 3 or 4 pine nuts.

Garnish the tops of the remaining squares with a slice of *cambozola*, a strip of roasted red pepper and a clove of garlic each.

Place the garnished *crostini* back under a hot broiler for 30 seconds or just until the cheese melts... watch them carefully. Remove them from the heat and arrange the *crostini* on serving trays (if serving as finger food) or individual plates and serve them immediately.

To roast a head of garlic

Remove the outermost layers of papery skin from the garlic (leaving a few layers intact). Slice or cut off the dry roots on the bottom of the bulb so that it sits flat. Turn the bulb on its side on a cutting board and carefully slice 1/2" (12 mm) off of the top of the bulb to partially expose the cloves.

Place the prepared bulb in a small glass or earthenware baking dish, drizzle 1 tsp. (5 l) of olive oil over the top and cover the dish with tin foil or a lid. Bake it in a 350° F (180° C) oven for approximately 30–40 minutes (depending on the size of the cloves), uncover it and bake for a further 10–15 minutes or until the cloves are soft but not mushy.

The roasted garlic head can be served whole and spread over crackers or thin toasted slices of bread by each diner, or separated into cloves, peeled and used as a garnish or mashed and used as a spread. Allow the bulb to cool slightly before separating and peeling the cloves.

Polenta croutons

makes about 60 croutons

2 garlic cloves, minced

1 Tbsp. (15 ml) extra virgin olive oil

2 cups (500 ml) cold water

1 tsp. (5 ml) salt

1/2 cup (125 ml) coarsely ground cornmeal

1 tsp. (5 ml) butter

1/4 cup (60 ml) freshly grated *parmigiano* cheese

freshly ground pepper

2 Tbsp. (30 ml) minced fresh Italian parsley

1 Tbsp. (15 ml) butter

1 Tbsp. (15 ml) safflower or vegetable oil

In a medium pot, sauté the garlic cloves in the olive oil at medium heat for 3–4 minutes or just until softened. Add the water and salt to the pot, then drizzle in the cornmeal, stirring it to prevent lumps from forming. Turn the heat to high, continue stirring and when the mixture starts to boil, reduce the temperature so that a very gentle bubbling is maintained.

Add the butter and continue stirring and cooking for 25 minutes or until the mixture is thick enough for the spoon to stand up in it for 3 or 4 seconds and the *polenta* grains lose their grittiness. If it gets too thick too early in the cooking process, add a little more water.

At the end of the cooking process, stir in the *parmigiano* cheese, a few grindings of fresh pepper and the parsley just before removing the *polenta* from the heat.

Pour it into an 8" x 8" (20 cm x 20 cm) lightly greased pan and spread it into a 3/4" (2 cm) layer. Let the *polenta* cool, then cut the cooled *polenta* into 1" x 1/2" (2.5 x 12 mm) croutons.

In a medium sauté pan, heat the butter and safflower oil to medium high. Fry the *polenta* croutons 10 or 12 at a time for 8 to 10 minutes until they are crispy and golden along the edges. Lift and turn them carefully with a lifter to keep them from sticking or losing their shape. (Be careful... the oil will splatter).

Remove the croutons to a rack lined with absorbent paper and gently rotate them a few times on the paper to soak up the oil. Keep the croutons warm, uncovered, in a low oven until you are ready to serve them on a tossed salad or on top of a hearty soup such as lentil or *minestrone*.

Making fresh pasta

ONE OF OUR BEST-LOVED WEDDING GIFTS was the manual pasta machine from Uncle Ernie and Aunty Pat. After more than 25 years of use, it looks the same as it did the first time we used it. The design has remained largely unchanged from the machine Nonna used—three sets of stainless steel rollers, side-by-side, turned by a removable handle inserted into a slot at the end of each set. The space between the rollers is adjusted by a dial which runs from 1 (widest) to 7. Running the hand-kneaded pasta dough through the widest setting two or three times continues the kneading process and

Giovanna Pascasi hand-cuts a fresh batch of fettucine in Antrodoco

helps to create a silky pasta with a consistent texture. As the pasta is run through progressively higher settings, it becomes thinner and longer.

Pasta can be hand-rolled and then sliced into the desired shape if you don't have a machine. However, a machine is a modest investment by kitchen equipment standards and makes the process quicker, easier, and therefore likely to happen more frequently! (Hand-operated pasta machines should never be exposed to water. To clean them after use, set the rollers to the widest width and brush off any residual flour. Store the machine in a dry location.)

Whenever Nonna made a batch of fresh pasta, she always treated her kitchen helpers with 3 or 4 squares which we put on top of the hot wood-burning stove. The heat caused the pasta squares to bubble up and turn into crispy little mouthfuls. In the absence of a wood-burning stove, we now toast the squares in the microwave for a minute or in a hot cast-iron pan—the result is not quite the same but it's close.

Basic pasta

This basic pasta recipe can be doubled or tripled. The amount of water you will need depends on the size of the eggs.
I follow Nonna's tradition of saving half an eggshell to scoop up and sprinkle the water.

3 large eggs, at room temperature
3 cups (750 ml) unbleached flour
a pinch of salt
approximately 1/2 cup (250 ml)
    cold water

Sift the flour and salt into a large wide bowl. Create a well in the centre of the flour mixture and crack in the eggs, saving one half-eggshell (washed) as a water measure.

With a fork, beat the eggs and gradually incorporate the flour into the eggs. When the mixture becomes too stiff to mix with a fork, continue mixing it with clean, dry hands. Add water sparingly, one eggshell measure at a time and mix in well after each addition. Add just enough water to create a stiff dough which incorporates all of the flour but is not sticky.

Knead the dough for 8–10 minutes, then let it rest in the bowl covered with a clean tea towel for 15 minutes.

Cut the dough into pieces the size of a large egg and shape each piece into a flat oblong of consistent thickness so that it will flatten uniformly in the pasta machine rollers.

Set the rollers on the pasta machine at the widest setting. (If you do not have a pasta machine, you can use a rolling pin – it's hard work but it works.) Roll each piece through at this setting twice. Then adjust the setting to the next level and roll each piece through again. Continue at progressively higher settings until the pasta is the desired thinness (for example, thinner for *lasagna*; thicker for *linguine*).

Lay the rolled pasta out on a cloth-covered table and let it dry slightly for 15–20 minutes. Cut the pieces into the desired shapes for the pasta dish you are making.

Maccheroni alla chitarra

GUITAR-CUT PASTA

serves 4–6

Maccheroni alla chitarra *are a specialty from the Abruzzo region.*
They are so-named because they are traditionally made by rolling a sheet of pasta (made with just egg and flour, no water)
slightly thicker than normal and then forcing it through a chitarra, *a set of closely strung strings that resemble the strings of a guitar.*
The result is square rather than round spaghetti.

Virtually the same effect can be achieved using a manual pasta machine by rolling the pasta to a thickness
equal to the width between the spaghetti-cutting blades, then running the pasta sheets through the blades
to cut them into noodles. These square home-made noodles are often served with meatballs (see Spaghetti con polpette).

2 1/2 cups (625 ml) flour
1 tsp. (5 ml) salt
4 large eggs
your choice of tomato or meat sauce
    or meatballs

Mix the salt into the flour, then mound the flour in a large wide bowl or on a clean, dry work surface.

Create a well in the centre of the flour mixture and crack in the eggs. With a fork, beat the eggs and gradually incorporate some of the flour into the eggs. When the mixture becomes too stiff to mix with a fork, continue incorporating the remaining flour with clean, dry hands. Knead the dough for 8–10 minutes.

Cut the dough into pieces the size of a large egg and shape each piece into a flat oblong of consistent thickness so that it will flatten uniformly in the pasta machine rollers.

Set the rollers on the pasta machine at the widest setting. Proceed to roll out the pasta as in the Basic Pasta recipe, rolling it to a thickness the width of the *spaghetti*-cutting blades (approximately the thickness of a quarter).

Lay it out on a covered table to dry for about 20 minutes, then run each strip through the spaghetti-cutting blades. Just before serving, cook the pasta in boiling salted water until *al dente*, drain it well and serve it with your choice of sauce.

Making tomato sauce

*Tomato sauce is a staple in many Abruzzese dishes
so it is a good idea to have some on hand at all times!*

Some hints for making a good tomato sauce –

❖ use good quality (fresh or canned) peeled
tomatoes. If using canned tomatoes, select
brands that have a deeply flavoured dense
pulp and fewer seeds, such as *San Marzano*
and *Italissima*;

❖ remove the seeds – they can add bitterness to
the sauce. To remove seeds, slice the tomato
in half and press out the seeds with your
thumb or a small spoon;

❖ add salt to the tomatoes when you begin
the cooking process rather than at the
end—the salt brings out the flavour
of the tomatoes while they cook;

❖ if you want to sweeten tomato sauce, add a
finely grated or minced carrot when you add the tomatoes to the pot;

❖ let tomato sauce cook at a gently bubbling simmer
for at least 25 minutes or until the consistency changes
to an integrated saucy texture.

*J.J. and Lucca Poscente
help Nonno Julio
preserve the tomatoes
for sauce.*

Basic tomato sauce

makes 7–8 cups (1.75–2 l) of sauce

This recipe can be doubled or tripled and freezes well.

2 Tbsp. (30 ml) extra virgin olive oil

one medium onion, finely chopped

one garlic clove, crushed and minced

5 lbs. (2.5 kg) fresh ripe plum tomatoes, peeled, seeded and roughly chopped **or** three 28 oz. (796 ml) tins plum tomatoes, seeds removed and pulp roughly chopped

1 large carrot, peeled and finely grated or minced (optional)

1 pinch chilli pepper flakes (optional)

salt and freshly ground pepper

3 Tbsp. (45 ml) chopped fresh basil **or** 1 Tbsp. (15 ml) *pesto di basilico* **or** 4 tsp. (20 ml) dried basil

In a saucepan large enough to hold all of the ingredients, sauté the oil and onion together for 8–10 minutes at medium heat until the onion is translucent and golden. Add the garlic and sauté for a further 4–5 minutes.

Add the tomatoes, minced carrot (if you want a sweeter taste), hot chilli pepper (if you like a sauce with a bite), 2 tsp. (10 ml) of salt and a generous grinding of black pepper and bring everything to a gentle bubbling simmer for 25–30 minutes. Stir the sauce occasionally and press the tomatoes against the sides of the pot to break down any large pieces.

Add the basil and cook for a further 8–10 minutes, then taste it and correct for seasoning with salt and pepper. If you prefer a smooth consistency, the sauce can be pressed through a sieve or lightly blended at this point.

Use the sauce immediately or cool and store it in airtight containers in the fridge for up to 5 days or freeze it for up to 3 months.

*Rich in antioxidant vitamins, tomatoes are a healthy,
versatile and delicious staple in Abruzzese cooking.*

*Uncle Julio proudly displays his tomato preserves, which
will be used over the winter months in sauces and soups.*

(See Basic tomato sauce, *page 38.)*

Two practised cooks make fresh fettucini...

Cousin Giovanna Pascasi **(ABOVE)** *cuts the pasta by hand in her Antrodoco home while Uncle Dante* **(RIGHT)** *guides the silky, wide noodles as they emerge from his pasta maker in Toronto.*

(See Making fresh pasta, *page 34.)*

Basic sugo

TOMATO MEAT SAUCE

makes 7–8 cups (1.75–2 l) of sauce

*Just as Nonna developed her own "signature" sugo or ragu, each of us has experimented over the years
to create our own family favourite. Uncle Julio adds a pinch of cinnamon;
I like the flavour of adding some hot Italian sausage to the ground meat.*

3 Tbsp. (45 ml) extra virgin olive oil

1 medium onion, minced

1 clove garlic, crushed and minced

2 lbs. (1 kg) of ground meat, using a
 mixture of two or three varieties
 (ground turkey, hot Italian sausage,
 lean ground beef, ground pork, or
 ground veal)

1 Tbsp. (15 ml) *pesto* **or** 1/2 tsp. (3 ml)
 each dried oregano, basil and
 rosemary

salt and freshly ground pepper

1/2 cup (125 ml) white wine

2 Tbsp. (30 ml) tomato paste, mixed
 with 1/4 cup (60 ml) beef or chicken
 broth

1 medium carrot, peeled and finely
 grated or minced

4 cups (1 l) Basic tomato sauce *(page 38)*

In a large pot, sauté the onion in the olive oil for 8–10 minutes, then add the garlic and sauté for a further 2–3 minutes.

Add the ground meats and break down any large clumps with a wooden spoon to achieve a uniform consistency. Add the *pesto* or dried herbs, 1 tsp. (5 ml) salt and a few generous grindings of pepper and cook over medium heat, stirring frequently and breaking down any lumps, until no pink remains in the meat.

Drain off and discard any liquid, then return the pan to the stovetop, add the white wine and cook at medium high heat until the wine is reduced by half. Add the tomato paste mixture and minced carrot and cook until the liquid is reduced by half.

Add the tomato sauce and simmer, uncovered, for 2 1/2–3 hours, stirring occasionally. Taste and adjust for salt and pepper halfway through the cooking process.

Use the sauce immediately over your choice of pasta, use it to assemble *lasagna* or cool it completely and store it in airtight containers in the freezer for up to 3 months.

Basic ragu con stracotto

SAUCE MADE WITH SLOW-COOKED BEEF

serves 6–8

This recipe uses a pot roast as the meat base for the sauce. The roast is slow-cooked for several hours with the sauce, and then shredded into tender, bite-sized pieces. The sauce takes on a deep, rich taste as it simmers with the meat. It is delicious over polenta, gnocchi or a sturdy pasta, such as rigatoni or bucatini.

1/4 cup (60 ml) extra virgin olive oil

2 1/2 lb. (1.25 kg) boneless cross rib roast, rolled and tied

2 cups (500 ml) dry red wine

2 garlic cloves, crushed and finely chopped

1 large onion, finely chopped

2 large carrots, finely chopped

3 celery stalks, trimmed and finely chopped

two 28 oz. (796 ml) tins plum tomatoes, seeded, chopped and drained, reserving liquid

2 large bay leaves

salt and freshly ground black pepper

Heat the oil to medium high in a large, heavy pot and brown the meat all over in the hot oil. When it has browned, pour in the wine and continue cooking until the wine is slightly reduced.

Add the garlic, onion, carrots, celery, and the tomatoes without the reserved liquid. Add the bay leaves, 1 tsp. (5 ml) salt and a few generous grindings of pepper, cover the pot and cook it over low heat at a gentle bubble for one hour, stirring occasionally and turning the roast over halfway through the cooking process.

After one hour of cooking, add one-half of the reserved liquid from the tomatoes and continue cooking, covered, for two more hours. Stir the sauce periodically and turn the roast so that all sides spend some time in the sauce. As the sauce starts to thicken and cook down, add more of the reserved tomato liquid.

After two hours, remove the roast from the pot with a slotted spoon and set it on a cutting board. Remove the bay leaves and discard them, then taste and adjust the sauce for salt and pepper.

Using a hand-held or stationary blender, blend the sauce for a few seconds. (If you do not have access to a blender, the sauce can be pressed through a strainer.)

Scrape off and discard any residual fat or connective tissue remaining on the roast. Slice the meat into thick pieces and then shred the slices into bite-sized pieces. Mix the shredded meat with the sauce and simmer for a few minutes longer.

Use the sauce on top of *polenta*, *gnocchi* or pasta and finish with grated cheese or cool the sauce completely and freeze in an airtight container for up to 3 months.

Basic balsamella sauce

BÉCHAMEL SAUCE

makes 2 cups

This easy to prepare basic white sauce can be used in baked pasta dishes such as lasagna *and* stracci.

4 Tbsp. (60 ml) butter
4 Tbsp. (60 ml) flour
2 cups (.5 l) 1%, 2% or homogenized
    milk, heated
pinch of nutmeg (optional)
salt and white pepper

Melt the butter in a saucepan. Whisk in the flour and cook over medium heat for 1 minute, just until it begins to bubble but not brown.

Add the heated milk and cook, whisking constantly, until the mixture thickens enough to coat the whisk. Remove it from the heat, add a pinch of nutmeg (optional), salt and pepper to taste.

Use *balsamella* in preparing *lasagna* or *stracci* or grate in some *parmigiano* or *fontina* cheese and use it as a simple white sauce over *fettucini*.

Bucatini all'Amatriciana

BUCATINI AMATRICE-STYLE

serves 4–6

*Amatrice, a town on the western side of the border between Lazio and Abruzzo, is the home of
this spicy and easy to prepare dish which uses the tube-shaped* bucatini, *a popular pasta shape in Abruzzese cooking.*
Pancetta *is a cured meat similar to bacon but salted, not smoked. It is available in most Italian markets.*

3 Tbsp. (45 ml) extra virgin olive oil

8 oz. (250 g) *pancetta*, sliced into 1/2"
(1.2 cm) thick slices and then diced
(do not substitute bacon)

2 garlic cloves, crushed and minced

1 medium onion, minced

1 pinch hot chilli pepper (or leave it
whole and remove it before serving)

2 lb. (1 k.) fresh ripe plum tomatoes,
peeled, seeded, roughly chopped **or**
two 28 oz. (796 ml) tin plum
tomatoes, seeds removed, pulp
roughly chopped

salt and freshly ground pepper

9 or 10 fresh basil leaves, torn

1 lb. (500 g) *bucatini*

salted water for boiling the pasta

1 cup (250 ml) grated *pecorino* or
parmigiano cheese

Heat the olive oil in a large saucepan over medium heat. Add the *pancetta* and cook, stirring often, until it is browned (about 10 minutes). Remove the *pancetta* with a slotted spoon, drain it on absorbent paper and reserve.

Add the onion to the pan and sauté it 6–8 minutes, until translucent. Add the garlic and sauté 2–3 minutes longer. Add the chilli pepper, tomatoes, a pinch of salt, a few generous grindings of pepper, the basil and the reserved *pancetta*, bring everything to a simmer and cook it uncovered, stirring occasionally, until the sauce thickens (about 25 minutes). The sauce can be made ahead to this point and reheated before serving.

To cook the *bucatini*, bring a large pot of salted water to a boil and drop in the *bucatini*. Cook, uncovered, over high heat, stirring periodically, for approximately 8 minutes, until the *bucatini* are *al dente*.

Drain, then transfer the *bucatini* to a warm serving platter, ladle the sauce over the *bucatini*, toss gently and top with a generous sprinkle of grated cheese. Serve immediately.

Tagliatelle con burro

FRESH-CUT NOODLES WITH BUTTER

serves 4

Fresh pasta has such a comforting, perfect taste and texture that it can stand on its own with the simplest of sauces.
Nonna often prepared an extra bowl of pasta with butter and cheese for the younger diners,
because even the pickiest ones couldn't resist it. The challenge for the children was to eat it before the adults got to it!

1/4 lb. (125 g) butter

2 garlic cloves, minced (optional)

1 batch of fresh pasta, cut into *tagliatelle* (1/4" or 6 mm. widths)

1/2 cup (125 ml) freshly grated *parmigiano* or *romano* cheese

1/4 cup (60 ml) chopped fresh Italian parsley

1/4 cup (60 ml) pine nuts, lightly toasted (optional)

salt and freshly ground pepper

Melt the butter in a large pot over low heat. If using, add the minced garlic and sweat it gently for 2–3 minutes.

While the butter is melting, cook the pasta in a large pot of rapidly boiling salted water until *al dente*, then drain it well.

Put the drained *tagliatelle* into the melted butter pot and toss to coat. Add the parsley, cheese, pine nuts and a few grindings of pepper and toss again. Serve immediately.

Lasagna

serves 10–12

Preparing lasagna *from scratch the way Nonna taught us is not for the faint of heart. It is best tackled by more than one set of hands and it occupies the better part of a day to prepare and assemble all of the elements. It is, however, a satisfying day filled with irresistible smells and the rewarding sounds of sighs as friends and family take that first bite.*

Nonna always made her lasagna *with fresh pasta, rolled thin and cooked in boiling water before being stacked in numerous layers alternately with thin layers of sauce and grated cheese. The result is very different from the* lasagna *which has become such a common menu feature in North American restaurants and delis. I like to add a layer of* balsamella *and spinach halfway up the stacking process for a little bit of extra creaminess and variety for the taste buds.*

If making an extra lasagna *(or two) for the freezer it should be frozen unbaked and allowed to thaw completely before baking.*

1 batch of Basic Pasta dough (p. 35), rolled very thinly (about the thickness of three sheets of paper)

1 batch of Basic tomato sauce (p. 38)

1 batch of Basic *Sugo* sauce (p. 39)

1 batch of Basic *Balsamella* sauce (p. 41)

one bunch of spinach leaves, steamed, chopped and drained well **or** one small package of frozen chopped spinach, cooked according to directions, drained well and seasoned with salt and freshly ground pepper

1 cup (250 ml) freshly grated *parmigiano* cheese

2 cups (500 ml) grated *mozzarella* cheese

1 cup (250 ml) grated *fontina* cheese

To cut the pasta: After the final rolling, lay the pieces out on a clean, dry flat surface and let them rest for 15 minutes. Then carefully slice each strip into 10" (24 cm) lengths, and cover them with a cloth until you are ready to boil them and assemble the *lasagna*.

To assemble the lasagna: Butter two 10" x 15" (25 cm x 39 cm) casserole dishes. Mix the cooked spinach with the *balsamella* and add a pinch of nutmeg. Set it aside. Arrange the dishes and the various sauces on your work counter for ease of assembly: bowls of *parmigiano, mozzarella* and *fontina* cheese, a pot of Basic tomato sauce, a pot of Basic *sugo* sauce, the *balsamella* spinach mixture, and a holding bowl for the cooked pasta.

Bring a large pot of salted water to a boil (a pasta pot with a colander insert is ideal). Place 7 or 8 pieces of pasta in the boiling water at a time and boil until just *al dente* (approximately 2 minutes). Do not overcook as the pasta will continue to cook as it bakes.

Lift the cooked pasta out of the pot with the colander insert or use a slotted spoon to lift the pasta and transfer it to a colander. Rinse the cooked pasta in cold water to stop the cooking process and drain it well, then put it in the holding bowl with a little bit of olive oil to prevent sticking while you are assembling the *lasagna*. Place the next 7 or 8 pieces of uncooked pasta in the boiling water and repeat this process until all of the pasta pieces are cooked.

As the pasta cooks, start assembling the *lasagna*, beginning with a thin layer of tomato sauce on the bottom of each casserole dish, a light sprinkle of *parmigiano*, then a layer of cooked pasta, a thin layer of *sugo* topped with a sprinkle of the *mozzarella* and a layer of pasta.

Repeat this pattern for another three layers, then do a layer of the balsamella and spinach with a sprinkling of *fontina* cheese, cover with pasta and continue to layer in the original pattern, ending with a layer of *sugo*.

Slice the last 7 or 8 cooked pasta pieces into 1/2" (12 mm) strips and use them to decorate the top of each *lasagna* with a lattice design. Moisten the lattice with tomato sauce and top it with whatever cheese remains.

The *lasagna* can be prepared ahead up to this point and refrigerated, covered, (or frozen) until you are ready to bake and serve it. (Frozen *lasagna* should be thawed before baking).

To bake the *lasagna*, cover the *lasagna* casseroles with foil and bake at 325° F (160° C) for 35–40 minutes. Remove the foil and bake them for another 10–15 minutes, until the cheese is bubbling and golden.

Remove the *lasagna* from the oven and let them sit for a few minutes. Slice the *lasagna* into serving portions and serve immediately.

Spaghettini alla carrottiera

SPAGHETTINI WITH GARLIC TOMATO SAUCE

serves 4

"Put on a bib e poi, buon appetito!" says Uncle Julio about this intensely flavoured and easy to prepare pasta dish. The recipe calls for spaghettini *but the sauce is also a robust counterpoint to the mildly flavoured* ravioli *with cheese filling.*

1 1/2–2 cups (375–500 ml) fresh basil
    leaves

5 or 6 large garlic cloves, finely minced

one 28 oz. (796 ml) can of plum
    tomatoes, seeded, drained and
    coarsely chopped

1/2 cup (125 ml) extra virgin olive oil

1 lb. (500 g) dried *spaghettini*

salt and freshly ground pepper

Finely chop the basil, then put the basil, garlic, tomatoes and oil in a saucepan, add salt to taste and a generous grinding of pepper and bring everything to a high simmer for about 25–30 minutes, stirring occasionally.

Warm a serving bowl and have it ready for the pasta. Bring a large pot of salted water to a boil, put in the pasta and cook it until it is *al dente*. Drain it well and put it into the warmed serving bowl.

Spoon the sauce over the pasta, gently toss to coat and serve immediately.

Spaghetti con polpette
SPAGHETTI AND MEATBALLS

serves 4–6

*Spaghetti and meatballs—a dish which has become so strongly associated with Italian cooking—
is a much more common dish outside of Italy than in Italy. Nevertheless, there are few better comfort foods than
a steaming platter of pasta smothered in a rich tomato sauce and crowned with juicy plump meatballs.
Nonna always used two kinds of ground meat to give a more interesting flavour and a smooth texture to the meatballs.*

1 lb. (500 g) lean ground veal or
 ground turkey

1/2 lb. (250 g) ground pork

2 eggs, lightly beaten

1/2 cup (125 ml) dried bread crumbs

1 tsp. (5 ml) salt

a few grindings of pepper

1/2 medium onion, finely minced

1 garlic clove, crushed and finely
 minced

1 Tbsp. (15 ml) finely chopped fresh
 Italian parsley

2 tsp. (10 ml) *pesto di verdure* **or**
 1 tsp. (5 ml) dried Italian herbs

1 Tbsp. (15 ml) *conserva* or tomato
 paste

1/4 cup (60 ml) chicken or beef broth

1 batch of Basic tomato sauce (p. 38)

1 batch of *maccheroni alla chitarra* **or**
 1 lb. (500 g) dried *spaghetti*

freshly grated *parmigiano* or *romano*
 cheese

Preheat the oven to 350° F (180° C).

Place all of the ingredients, except the tomato sauce, pasta and cheese, in a large
bowl and, using a large fork or clean hands, mix well to combine.

Roll the mixture into golf-ball sized balls and arrange them on an oiled baking
pan so they do not touch. Place the pan in a hot oven and bake the meatballs for
10 minutes.

Remove the pan from the oven, loosen the meatballs with a lifter then gently shake
the pan to rotate the meatballs. Return the pan to the oven and bake the meatballs
for a further 15 minutes.

While the meatballs are baking, put the tomato sauce in a pot large enough to
comfortably hold all of the meatballs and place it over medium heat. Using a slotted
spoon, lift the cooked meatballs into the tomato sauce and let the mixture simmer
for 1 1/2–2 hours. (The sauce and meatballs can be prepared ahead up to this point
and refrigerated or frozen in an airtight container until ready to reheat and serve).

Just before serving, cook the pasta in a large pot of boiling salted water until
al dente. Drain it well, pour it into a warmed serving bowl or platter.

Spoon 3/4 of the sauce over and gently toss to coat the pasta. Top it with half of the
meatballs and place the remaining meatballs in a separate, warmed serving bowl so
that people can help themselves to extras. Top both bowls with a generous sprinkle
of grated cheese and serve immediately.

Stracci

ABRUZZESE CREPES

serves 6–8

Stracci, which translates literally as "little rags", is a regional specialty of Abruzzo and a delicious alternative to pasta. "Stracci" are thin crepes which are rolled up around a tomato-meat filling or a meatless filling and baked in a tomato or meat sauce. Some of Nonna's children and grandchildren like to add a light drizzle of balsamella sauce or grated fontina cheese for extra moistness and taste—an adaptation of which I think Nonna would have approved! Making stracci involves preparing the meat and/or meatless filling(s), the sauces, and the crepes, then assembling and baking the filled crepes.

Meat filling

2 Tbsp. (30 ml) extra virgin olive oil

3/4 lb. (375 g) lean ground veal or beef

3/4 lb. (375 g) ground pork

salt and freshly ground pepper

2 tsp. (10 ml) *pesto di verdure* **or**
    1/2 tsp. (2 ml) each dried oregano and thyme

1 cup (250 ml) Basic tomato sauce

Spinach and *Ricotta* filling:

3/4 lb. (375 g) fresh spinach leaves, cooked in
    salted water, well-drained and finely chopped **or**
    one 10 oz. (315 g) package of frozen chopped
    spinach, cooked according to package
    directions, drained well and chopped finely

8 oz. (250 g) *ricotta* cheese, drained

1/2 cup (125 ml) grated *pecorino* cheese

2 egg yolks, lightly beaten

3 or 4 grindings of black pepper

a pinch of ground nutmeg

grated *romano* or *parmigiano* cheese

To prepare the meat filling:

Heat the olive oil to medium and sauté the ground meats, stirring to break up any clumps, until all pink has disappeared.

Drain off any fluids, add seasoning and salt and pepper to taste. Add just enough Basic tomato sauce to moisten the meat but not make it runny (approximately 1 cup/250 ml) and let this mixture simmer for half an hour. Set aside.

To prepare the Spinach and *Ricotta* filling:

Mix all of the ingredients with a fork until they are well-blended. Set aside.

Stracci

Continued

The sauces

4 cups (1 l) Basic tomato sauce

2 cups (.5 l) of Basic *balsamella* sauce **or**
  1 1/2 cups (375 ml) grated *mozzarella*
  or *fontina* cheese

1 cup (250 ml) freshly grated *romano* or
  parmigiano cheese

The crepes

8 eggs, cracked and measured in a liquid
  measuring cup

1 tsp. (5 ml) salt

the same amount of water as eggs

2 cups (500 ml) flour (approximately)

Prepare the sauces according to directions (tomato sauce p. 38, *balsamella* p. 41), grate the cheese(s) and set aside.

To prepare the crepes:

Beat the eggs and salt in a large bowl or use a blender. Gradually add the water and continue beating until well blended.

Add the flour a few tablespoons at a time, beating to incorporate the flour after each addition to prevent lumps from forming. Add just enough flour to make a pourable crepe-like consistency (thinner than pancake batter but thick enough to coat a spoon well). Let the batter sit for a few minutes.

Grease a crepe pan or 8" (20 cm) non-stick pan and heat it to medium. Holding the heated pan in one hand, pour 1/4 cup (60 ml) of the batter into the pan and quickly tip the pan in a circular motion to evenly distribute the batter before it starts to get firm. The crepe should be about 6" (15 cm) in diameter and as thin as possible.

Return the pan to the heat, cook the crepe lightly on one side and carefully turn it over to cook the other side briefly. Remove the crepe to a plate, cover it with a clean towel and continue making and stacking crepes until all the batter has been used. (The crepes can also be made with a crepe pan, following the same procedure as for making crepes.)

Continued on next page

Stracci

Continued

Niki Poscente
displays her
stracci.

***To fill and assemble* the stracci**
Butter two 10" x 15" (25 x 39 cm) casserole dishes and spread a thin layer of the Basic tomato sauce on the bottom of each dish.

Lay a crepe on a clean dry work surface and distribute a heaping tablespoon of filling in a line across the centre of the crepe. Drizzle a little *balsamella* sauce or a pinch of grated *mozzarella* or *fontina* cheese over the filling, tuck one side of the crepe around the filling, then roll over the other side to create a log shape. Arrange the filled crepes side-by-side in one layer in the casserole dish (they should nestle up against each other but not overlap).

Once all of the crepes have been used, spoon the remaining tomato sauce over both dishes of *stracci* and spread gently to distribute, adjusting the crepes to allow some of the sauce to drip down between them.

Drizzle the remaining *balsamella* sauce over both dishes (don't spread it) or sprinkle them with the remaining *mozzarella* or *fontina*. Finish with a generous sprinkle of grated *romano* or *parmigiano*. The *stracci* can be prepared ahead up to this point and refrigerated, covered, for several hours before baking and serving.

Bake the *stracci*, covered, in a preheated 325° F (160° C) oven for 20 minutes, remove the cover and bake for a further 15–20 minutes. The *balsamella* and cheese should be bubbling. Let the *stracci* set for a few minutes and serve them by carefully lifting the *stracci* rolls on to individual plates with a lifter.

Sumptuous displays of fresh produce in Italy make shopping for dishes like peperonata *(see page 94) or* peperoni imbottiti *(see page 92) a visual treat.*

Editor Lindsay Sovran Mitchell rolls out a batch of dough for a big pasta feast with friends in Halifax—a welcome break from university studies and cafeteria food.

(See Lasagna, page 44, and Ravioli, page 52.)

Ravioli

FILLED PASTA POCKETS

makes about 4 dozen

Ravioli *take time to assemble and making them works best*
when there is more than one set of hands to help.
The recipe can be doubled or tripled and the ravioli can be frozen, uncooked.
There is a wide range of possible fillings for ravioli, in addition to the two options which follow.

Ravioli with meat filling

3 Tbsp. (45 ml) butter

1/4 cup (60 ml) very finely minced onion

1 garlic clove, crushed and very finely minced

3/4 lb. (375 g) finely ground veal or ground turkey breast

3/4 lb. (375 g) fresh spinach leaves, cooked, very well-drained and finely chopped **or** one 10 oz. (315 g) package of frozen chopped spinach, cooked according to package directions, drained very well and chopped finely

1/2 cup (125 ml) freshly grated *parmigiano* cheese

1 tsp. (5 ml) *pesto di basilico* **or** 1/4 tsp. (1 ml) each dried oregano, basil and thyme

3 eggs, lightly beaten

salt and freshly ground pepper

one batch of Basic Pasta dough (p. 35), divided into four pieces, rolled to the thickness of a dime into long rectangular sheets and covered with a damp towel

3–4 cups (750 ml–1 l) of your choice of sauce

freshly grated *parmigiano* or *romano* cheese

Heat the butter in a large sauté pan and cook the onions and garlic for 8–10 minutes or until they are translucent and golden.

Add the ground veal or turkey and sauté, stirring constantly to break up any clumps and cook it evenly until no pinkness remains.

Drain the mixture in a colander for a few minutes and transfer it into a mixing bowl. Let it cool slightly, then stir in the chopped cooked spinach, *parmigiano*, *pesto* or herbs, and beaten eggs. Add salt and pepper to taste.

To fill the *ravioli*, place one sheet of pasta on the board and, using a teaspoon, place little mounds of the filling about 2" (5 cm) apart on the pasta, creating a checkerboard pattern of about 24 mounds.

Dip a small brush or your finger in water and make a grid of wet lines vertically and horizontally between the mounds of filling. This creates the "glue" to bond the bottom sheet of pasta to the top.

Carefully place a second sheet of pasta on top of the first one and press down firmly all along the moistened lines. Using a *ravioli* cutter, a pizza slicer or a pastry wheel (or simply a sharp knife if none of these is available), cut along the wet lines into small squares. Check each square to make sure that the edges are sealed.

Set the squares aside on a lightly floured surface or waxed paper and repeat the procedure with the other two sheets of pasta and the remaining filling. The *ravioli* can be prepared ahead to this point and either refrigerated or frozen until you are ready to cook and serve them.

Ravioli with Meat Filling

Continued

When you are ready to cook the *ravioli*, preheat the oven to 200° F (100° C). Place a lightly buttered serving platter in the oven to warm.

To cook the *ravioli*, drop them 8–10 at a time into a large pot of boiling salted water and stir them once or twice very gently with a wooden spoon to prevent them from sticking to each other or to the bottom of the pot.

Cook the *ravioli* for about 6 minutes or until they are *al dente*, drain them gently but thoroughly and set them in the warmed serving platter. Ladle on some sauce and toss gently to keep them from sticking while the remaining *ravioli* are cooked. Keep adding the cooked *ravioli* to the platter as they are ready, adding additional sauce as necessary.

When all of the *ravioli* are cooked, generously sprinkle the cheese over them and put the platter in the preheated oven for a few minutes to heat the *ravioli* through. Serve immediately.

Ravioli with cheese filling

1 cup (250 cc) *ricotta*, drained for
   1/2 hour in a colander set over
   a bowl and drained liquids discarded

1/2 cup (125 ml) grated *fontina* cheese

3/4 cup (185 ml) grated *parmigiano*
   cheese

2 tsp. (10 ml) finely minced onion

3 egg yolks, lightly mixed

a pinch of nutmeg

1 tsp. (5 ml) salt and a few grindings
   of pepper

In a large bowl, combine the *ricotta, fontina, parmigiano*, onion, egg yolks, nutmeg and salt and pepper and mix well.

Proceed to fill and cook the *ravioli* as for the directions in *Ravioli with Meat Filling.*

Gnocchi
TINY POTATO DUMPLINGS

serves 4–6

In **The Cooking of Italy,** *Waverly Root notes that* gnocchi *is one of the first traditions in Italian cuisine, dating back to the early Romans. One of the few traditional Italian dishes to feature potatoes,* gnocchi *means little dumplings, describing the characteristic shape. There are various regional variations and even within a region, Italian families have adapted their own recipes and techniques. Nonna made her* gnocchi *with potatoes, flour and eggs (although she remembered times from her childhood when they were made with just potatoes and flour).*

According to my sister, Lorraine, who has mastered Nonna's art, the key to making delicate gnocchi *is to keep the amount of moisture to a minimum, add as little flour as possible and do not overwork the dough. This means using old baking potatoes (new potatoes are too sticky), cooking the potatoes with a scant amount of water, or baking them..*

While Nonna usually served her gnocchi *with a simple tomato or meat sauce,* gnocchi *also pair well with many sauces, such as gorgonzola melted in a* balsamella *sauce, a simple pesto, or butter and sage.*

6 large old baking or russet potatoes (about 4 lbs. / 2 kg) The older and drier the potatoes, the better. Do not use new potatoes.

2 eggs

1 1/2 to 2 cups (325 ml–500 ml) flour

1 tsp. salt

a pot of salted water for boiling the *gnocchi*

Basic tomato sauce, Basic *Sugo*, or *Ragu con stracotto*, heated

grated *pecorino* or *romano* cheese

Preheat the oven to 350° F (180° C).

Wash and dry the potatoes, pierce them a few times with a fork to prevent them from exploding while cooking, then bake them until they are squeezable and fork tender, about 1 to 1 1/2 hours, depending on the size of the potatoes. Remove them from the oven and immediately slice into each potato, then squeeze both ends towards each other gently to create an opening from which the steam can escape.

When the potatoes are cool enough to handle, peel them, discard the peels (or use them to make baked potato skins) and put the peeled potatoes through a potato ricer or mash them well with a fork to eliminate any lumps.

While still warm, place the prepared potatoes on a large floured board, forming a mound with a well in the centre. Distribute the flour around the outside of the potatoes. Put the egg and the salt into the well. Beating the egg with a fork, incorporate the egg gradually into the potatoes.

Then, **mixing with your hands**, slowly start adding the flour a little at a time into the potato-egg mixture, and continue adding only enough of the flour to create a soft dough. Gently knead it very briefly until you have achieved a soft, smooth dough.

To shape the *gnocchi*, break off a handful of the dough, and roll the piece into a rope about the thickness of a finger. Cut the rope into approximately 1/2" (1.2 cm) pieces to create small, puffy cubes.

Gently press the middle of each cube, one by one, with your index finger, rolling the dough towards you as you press so that it flips over, creating a little oval dumpling with a small pocket on the underside. Move the rolled *gnocchi* to a floured surface on the board to rest while you roll the next ones.

Continue working the remaining dough in this manner. Place the prepared *gnocchi* on a lightly floured baking sheet and either cook them immediately, or cover and keep them refrigerated until ready to use, preferably not more than 3 hours.

When ready to serve, turn the oven to 200° F (100° C). Put a serving platter in the oven to warm.

To cook the *gnocchi*, bring a large pot of salted water to a boil. Carefully drop 12 to 15 *gnocchi* at a time into salted, boiling water and stir once with a wooden spoon to prevent them from sticking to each other. Remove the *gnocchi* with a slotted spoon as soon as they have floated to the surface (this usually takes less than a minute.) Drain and put the cooked *gnocchi* on the warmed serving platter.

Ladle on a little bit of hot sauce and gently toss to coat the *gnocchi*. Keep adding *gnocchi* to the platter as they are cooked, spooning on more sauce as necessary. When all of the *gnocchi* are cooked, top with a ladleful of sauce and generously sprinkle with freshly grated or shredded cheese.

Put the platter of *gnocchi* into the warmed oven for a few minutes to heat through and serve hot.

Basic risotto

ITALIAN ARBORIO RICE

serves 6

Risotto dishes follow a standard procedure of making a soffritto (fried mixture), usually including onions and garlic, in a mixture of butter and oil, then adding the uncooked arborio rice and sautéing briefly to coat all of the grains. The liquid is then added one cup at a time and cooked down, while the rice is constantly stirred. Other ingredients are added in the last stage of the cooking process. Nonna always added sugo or tomato sauce to her risotto but the possibilities are endless.

3 Tbsp. (45 ml) butter

1 Tbsp. (15 ml) extra virgin olive oil

1 small onion, minced

2 1/2 cups (625 ml) *arborio* rice (do not rinse). Do not substitute other types of rice.

1 cup (250 ml) dry white wine

8 cups (2 l) broth (chicken, beef, fish or vegetable) or consommé, heated

salt and freshly ground pepper

1/2 cup (125 ml) grated *parmigiano* or *romano* cheese

In a heavy pot, melt the butter and oil, add the onions and cook for 6–8 minutes, until the onions are translucent, but not brown.

Add the uncooked *arborio* rice and stir for a few minutes to completely coat the grains in the oil mixture.

Increase the heat to medium, add the white wine and cook it down until it is almost completely absorbed. Over the next 15 minutes or so, add the hot broth, approximately 3/4 cup (185 ml) at a time, stirring slowly and constantly. Allow the rice to almost fully absorb each addition of stock before adding the next cup.

The *risotto* is ready when it is creamy and the individual grains are tender but *al dente*. Adjust for salt and pepper and stir in grated cheese just before serving.

Nonna's risotto

Follow the Basic *risotto* recipe, using chicken stock, but replace the last cup (250 ml) of broth with 2 cups (500 ml) of *Sugo* (p. 39) or Basic tomato sauce (p. 38). Complete cooking as per the *risotto* recipe.

To serve, spread the *risotto* to an even thickness on individual heated plates (this helps it to maintain a consistent temperature) and sprinkle it with grated cheese. Serve immediately.

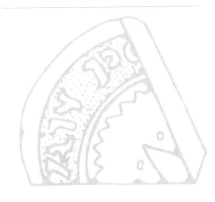

Risotto con asparagi
ASPARAGUS RISOTTO

serves 4–6

*There is something about the combination of asparagus and rice
which brings out the comforting characteristics of both ingredients. If young asparagus are not in season
and you are using the thicker, more mature spears, try cutting them in julienne strips.*

1 lb. (500 g) young asparagus spears, trimmed and sliced diagonally into 1" (2.5 cm) lengths
3 Tbsp. (45 ml) butter
1 Tbsp. (15 ml) extra virgin olive oil
1 small onion, minced
1 garlic clove, crushed and minced
2 1/2 cups (625 ml) *arborio* rice (do not rinse)
zest from one lemon
1 cup (250 ml) dry white wine
8 cups (2 l) broth (chicken or vegetable) or consommé, heated
salt and freshly ground pepper
1/2 cup (125 ml) grated *fontina* cheese

Parcook the asparagus spears in a small quantity of salted boiling water until tender but not soft. Drain and immerse them in cold water to arrest the cooking process. Drain them again and set them aside.

In a heavy pot, melt the butter and oil, add the onions and cook at medium heat for 6–8 minutes, add the garlic and cook for a further 3–4 minutes.

Add the rice and cook, stirring, for a few minutes to completely coat the grains. Stir in the lemon zest. Add the white wine, increase the heat to the boiling point and cook the wine down, stirring, until it is absorbed.

Over the next 15 minutes or so, add the hot broth, approximately 3/4 cup (185 ml) at a time, stirring slowly and constantly. Allow the rice to almost fully absorb the stock before adding the next cup. With the final addition of broth, add the steamed asparagus and continue stirring.

The *risotto* is ready when it is creamy and the individual grains are tender but *al dente*. Adjust for salt and pepper and stir in the grated cheese just before serving.

Risotto con cozze e zafferano

RISOTTO WITH MUSSELS AND SAFFRON

serves 6

For seafood lovers, this version of risotto is a delicious way to enjoy fresh mussels.
Mussels are used in coastal Abruzzese cuisine, and saffron, which adds a soft colour and subtle flavour to this dish,
grows in the mountainous interior of the Abruzzo region.

For the mussels:

1 cup (250 ml) white wine

1/2 cup (125 ml) water

2 shallots, thinly sliced

1 garlic clove, crushed

3 lb. (1.5 kg) mussels in their shells, cleaned and scrubbed very well

For the *risotto*:

3 Tbsp. (45 ml) butter

1 Tbsp. (15 ml) extra virgin olive oil

1 fennel bulb, sliced lengthwise into fine julienne strips

1 small onion, minced

1 garlic clove, crushed and minced

2 1/2 cups (625 ml) *arborio* rice

1 cup (250 ml) dry white wine

6 cups (1.5 l) fish stock, heated (see note)

3 or 4 saffron threads

salt and freshly ground pepper

To cook the mussels: Bring the white wine, water, shallots and garlic to a gentle boil in a pot large enough to hold the mussels. Add the mussels, cover and boil over a medium high heat until all of the shells have opened.

Drain the mussels through a fine sieve placed over a large bowl and reserve the juices and cooking liquid. Discard any unopened mussels. Leave 18 mussels in their shells and shell the remainder. Set both aside.

Add the reserved cooking liquid from the mussels to the fish stock to make 8 cups (2 l). (Top it up with water if necessary.) Add the saffron threads and heat the stock.

To cook the *risotto*: In a large heavy pot, sauté the fennel, onion and garlic in the butter and oil for 8–10 minutes until translucent. Add the rice and cook, stirring, for a few minutes. Proceed as in the Basic *risotto* recipe, adding first the white wine and then the hot fish stock, 3/4 cup at a time, stirring constantly until the *risotto* is creamy and *al dente*. After the last addition of stock has cooked down, add the shelled mussels and gently toss them to distribute and heat the mussels through. Taste and adjust for salt and pepper.

Serve the *risotto* in individual heated bowls, garnished with three mussels in their shells.

Note: Canned fish stock or clam nectar can be used or prepare the *Easy Fish Stock* on page 15.

Fish on Fridays

The Catholic tradition of meatless Fridays gave rise to a wide and creative range of dishes, many of which were rarely served on other days of the week. Fish or seafood or egg dishes replaced the usual meat course. Nonna even created a Friday version of spaghetti and "meatballs," using tuna instead of ground meat. One memorable Friday dinner to which the parish priest was invited, Nonna served a steaming platter of pasta tossed with a rich tomato sauce and crowned with the browned, round tuna balls. The platter apparently so closely resembled the meat version that the unsuspecting priest scolded Nonna for serving meat on Friday!

The interior of the Abruzzo region is lined with streams and rivers rich with trout. Nonna's adopted North American home, like her birthplace of Antrodoco, was inland. The main source of fish was trout from the freshwater streams, lakes and rivers. Cod, preserved in salt, was imported and used to make the intensely flavoured *bacala*. Occasionally, the seafood truck came to town loaded with fresh bounty from the coast and Nonna's kitchen would briefly be filled with the heady, sweet aroma of prawns simmering in white wine and tomatoes.

Fish, meat, poultry and egg recipes

Gamberi al pomodoro
PRAWNS SIMMERED IN TOMATOES

serves 4–6

*This is a messy and delectable way to enjoy fresh prawns. Don't wear white and make sure to have a good supply of napkins!
The prawns are best enjoyed by breaking off the tail portion, placing the whole head portion in your mouth
and sucking up the wonderful juice. Then discard this portion and suck the tail portion in the same way before peeling
and eating it. The ultimate prize is discovering a prawn in your bowl filled with roe (eggs) – squisito!*

4 Tbsp. (60 ml) extra virgin olive oil

1 large onion, finely chopped

3 garlic cloves, minced

1 small chilli pepper

two 28 oz. (796 ml) tins plum tomatoes,
seeds removed and roughly chopped

handful **each** of fresh basil, torn and
fresh Italian parsley, chopped

5 or 6 threads of saffron, crumbled

1 cup (250 ml) white wine

1/2 cup (125 ml) red vermouth

salt and freshly ground pepper to taste

4 –5 lbs. (2-2.25 kg) large fresh whole
prawns, in their shells

fresh Italian parsley for garnish

one lemon, sliced

In a large pot, sauté the onion and garlic in olive oil for 6–8 minutes or until translucent. Add the chilli pepper, tomatoes, basil, parsley, saffron, a generous pinch of salt and several grindings of black pepper.

Bring everything just to bubbling and cook for 25–30 minutes, stirring frequently and pressing tomato chunks against the side of the pot to break them up.

Remove and discard the chilli, add the wine and vermouth and let the sauce bubble for a few minutes. Add the prawns, whole, and simmer them in the sauce, stirring a few times, until they are pink and cooked through. (This should take 7–10 minutes, depending on the size of the prawns.)

Ladle the prawns and sauce into soup bowls, garnish with the remaining parsley and the lemon slices and serve.

Serving suggestion: Serve the *gamberi* with a hearty, crusty bread and follow with a light *insalata verde*.

Cioppino di Giulio
JULIO'S SEAFOOD SOUP

serves 4–6

Uncle Julio usually creates a big pot of this magnificent cioppino *whenever he visits the west coast. Nonna would have loved it!*

The choice of seafood can be varied, depending on seasonal availability.

2 cups (500 ml) chopped onions

1/2 cup (125 ml) chopped green pepper

6 garlic cloves, crushed and minced

1/2 cup (125 ml) extra virgin olive oil

one 5 1/2 oz. (156 ml) tin tomato paste

one 28 oz. (796 ml) tin plum tomatoes,
seeded and roughly chopped

1 cup (250 ml) dry red wine

1 cup (250 ml) sherry

one lemon, sliced

1 cup (250 ml) chopped fresh Italian
parsley, half of it set aside for garnish

1 Tbsp. (15 ml) each fresh basil and
oregano **or** 1 tsp. (5 ml) of each, dried

salt and freshly ground pepper

1 large or three small lobster tails, cut into
1" (2.5 cm) pieces

1 lb. (500 g) large shrimp or prawns,
shelled and deveined

20 clams, shells scrubbed cleaned

24 mussels, shells scrubbed clean

1 1/2 lb. (750 g) halibut, sliced into
2" (5 cm) wide slices

In a pot large enough to hold all of the ingredients, sauté the onions, green peppers, garlic and olive oil gently for 10 minutes. Add the remaining ingredients, except the seafood, and simmer for 25 minutes.

Add the lobster and simmer gently for 6–8 minutes, stirring periodically. Add the prawns, clams, mussels and halibut and simmer for a further 8–10 minutes, stirring carefully once or twice until the shells are open and the halibut is cooked through.

Discard any unopened clams or mussels.
Ladle the *cioppino* into individual soup bowls or a large soup tureen, garnish with the remaining parsley and serve it immediately with crusty bread for soaking up the juices.

Serving suggestion:
Follow with a crisp
insalata verde.

Trota con menta, capperi e acciughe

TROUT WITH MINT, CAPERS AND ANCHOVIES

serves 4–6

*The sweetness of mint, saltiness of anchovies and tartness of capers
create an intensely flavoured sauce to complement the mild tasting trout.*

3 large fresh trout, cleaned, deboned
and filleted into six pieces

1/2 cup (125 ml) flour, generously
seasoned with salt and pepper

6 Tbsp. (90 ml) safflower or vegetable oil

For the sauce:

3 Tbsp. (45 ml) butter

4 anchovy filets, cut into small pieces

1 cup (250 ml) white wine

1 Tbsp. (15 ml) **each** chopped capers,
chopped fresh mint and chopped
fresh Italian parsley

juice of 1/2 lemon

1 tsp. sugar

Preheat oven to 200° F (100° C). Put a serving platter in the oven to warm.

Dredge the trout fillets in the seasoned flour and shake off any excess. Heat the safflower oil to medium high in a large heavy pan and brown the fillets on both sides just until the trout is cooked through (the cooking time will vary, depending on the thickness of the trout). Place the fried fillets on the warmed platter and place the platter in the warm oven.

Melt the butter in a saucepan over a low heat. Add the cut up anchovy filets and sauté for five minutes, stirring frequently. Add the wine, increase the heat, bring it to a gentle boil and simmer for 5 minutes or until the wine is slightly reduced.

Add the capers, mint and parsley and simmer for 3 minutes, then add the lemon juice and sugar and simmer for another minute. Remove the saucepan from the heat, pour the sauce over the trout and serve hot.

Serving suggestion: This flavourful fish is good served with *risotto*.

Trota al forno

BAKED TROUT

serves 6

The two stage cooking process for the trout—pan-frying followed by baking—produces a beautifully tender and succulent texture.

1 Tbsp. (15 ml) butter
1 medium onion, thinly sliced
1 garlic clove, crushed and minced
4 fresh ripe large tomatoes, peeled, seeded and roughly chopped
a pinch of crushed chilli pepper
1 tsp. **each** dried oregano and thyme
2 Tbsp. (30 ml) chopped fresh Italian parsley
salt and freshly ground pepper

6 trout (individual serving size), cleaned, deboned and dried
1 cup (250 ml) flour, generously seasoned with salt and pepper
6 Tbsp. (90 ml) safflower or vegetable oil
juice of 1 lemon
1 lemon, sliced
fresh Italian parsley for garnish

In a medium-sized heavy saucepan, melt the butter, add the chopped onion and garlic and sauté over medium heat for 6–8 minutes until the onions are translucent. Add the chopped tomatoes, crushed chilli peppers, oregano, thyme, parsley and salt and pepper to taste and simmer everything for 25 minutes.

Preheat the oven to 325° F (160° C).

While the sauce is simmering, dredge the trout in the seasoned flour and shake off any excess. Heat the oil to medium high in a large heavy pan and brown the trout on all sides.

Place the browned trout in a buttered baking or casserole dish large enough that the fish touch but do not overlap. Drizzle them with lemon juice, pour the sauce evenly over them and scatter slices of lemon over all.

Bake for 20 minutes, uncovered and serve hot, garnished with chopped fresh Italian parsley.

Serving suggestion: Serve with wedges of grilled *polenta* and a side of *soffritto di spinaci e aglio.*

Involtini di vitello

VEAL BUNDLES

serves 6

These popular little bundles (sometimes called veal birds) can also be made with turkey breast sliced into scallopine.

1/2 cup (125 ml) bread crumbs

1/3 cup (80 ml) milk

1/4 lb. (125 g) *prosciutto*, finely diced

1 egg, lightly beaten

1/2 cup (125 ml) freshly grated *parmigiano*

salt and freshly ground pepper

1 Tbsp. (15 ml) chopped fresh parsley

1 tsp. chopped fresh sage

1 1/2 lbs. (750 g) top round veal **or** turkey breast cut across the grain into thin *scallopine* and pounded flat and very thin into 3" x 5" (7 cm x 13 cm) pieces

3/4 cup (180 ml) flour, seasoned with pepper

4 Tbsp. (60 ml) butter

2 Tbsp. (30 ml) safflower or vegetable oil

1/2 cup (125 ml) dry white wine

3/4 cup (180 ml) chicken or beef broth

fresh Italian parsley for garnish

Put a serving platter in a 200° F (100° C) oven to warm.

Soak the bread crumbs in milk and put them in a bowl with the *prosciutto*, egg, cheese, a few grindings of fresh pepper, parsley and sage. Mix thoroughly with your hands.

Lay the *scallopine* out flat. Place a rounded Tbsp (15 ml) of the bread crumb/*prosciutto* mixture in the centre of each *scallopine* and shape the mixture into a log. Roll the *scallopine* up snugly, tuck in the ends and secure with one or two toothpicks inserted lengthwise.

Put the seasoned flour on a plate. Dredge the rolls (*involtini*) in the seasoned flour, shake off any residual flour and set them on a plate.

Heat the butter and oil to medium high in a sauté pan large enough to hold the *involtini* in one layer. When the foam of the butter subsides, place the *involtini* in the hot oil/butter and brown them quickly on all sides.

Once they are browned, pour in the white wine and let it bubble for a few minutes, then add the broth and turn the *involtini* over in the broth wine mixture to moisten them. Reduce the heat to low, cover the pan and simmer gently for 20 to 25 minutes, turning the *involtini* again after about 10 minutes. Using a slotted spoon, lift the *involtini* onto the heated serving platter and carefully remove the toothpicks.

Gently whisk the cooking juices remaining in the pan. If the juices are too thick to pour, add a little bit of water and whisk together over a medium heat until they reach the desired consistency. (If the juices are too runny, turn up the heat and let them cook down to the desired consistency.)

Drizzle the juices over the *involtini*, garnish with parsley and serve hot.
Serving suggestion: serve with a side of *soffritto di spinaci e aglio*.

Spezzatini di vitello con limone

TINY BITES OF VEAL WITH LEMON

serves 4

The veal simmers slowly for more than an hour, producing tender little bite-sized morsels in a richly flavourful sauce.
The addition of lemon juice to finish adds a piquant bite.

2 Tbsp. (30 ml) extra virgin
 olive oil

1 Tbsp. (15 ml) butter

2.2 lbs. (1 kg) lean leg of veal,
 cut up into small bite-
 sized chunks

1 garlic clove, minced

1 sprig of rosemary

1 cup (250 ml) chicken broth

juice from 1 small lemon

salt and freshly ground pepper

Heat the olive oil and butter to medium high in a heavy sauté pan.

When the foam starts to subside, add the veal and stir slowly as it browns. Add the garlic, rosemary sprig and broth, cover, reduce the heat and let it simmer gently for 1 hour, stirring occasionally.

After an hour, remove the cover, remove and discard the rosemary sprig and cook any remaining juices down by half. Stir in the lemon juice and salt and pepper to taste and simmer for one minute. Serve hot.

Serving suggestion: Start with a basic *risotto* then serve the *spezzatini di vitello* with *soffritto di spinaci con aglio* or *peperone misti*.

Vitello indoratto

VEAL WITH LEMON AND EGGS

On Easter Sunday, after attending morning Mass at St. Anthony's Church, our family walked to Papa's and Nonna's house to share an Easter lunch tradition which Nonna experienced as a child in Antrodoco. The girls and women, resplendent in our new Easter bonnets, the men dressed up in suits and ties, arrived to the wonderful anisette aroma of toasted Pizza di Pasqua (Easter Bread) and the savoury lemon and rosemary scent of vitello indoratto .

same ingredients as for
 spezzatini di vitello (above)

2 eggs, well-beaten

Follow the same process as for *spezzatini di vitello* (above). ***However***, after adding the lemon, and just before serving, mix two well-beaten eggs with the simmered veal and let it cook just until the eggs are no longer runny. This unusual and delicious combination of flavours and textures makes it a tasty special occasion brunch dish.

Piccata al limone

VEAL AND LEMON

serves 4–6

2 1/4 lb. (1 kg) top round of veal, cut against the grain into thin *scallopine*

1 cup (250 ml) flour, seasoned with freshly ground pepper

4 Tbsp. (60 ml) extra virgin olive oil

6 Tbsp. (90 ml) butter

juice from two large lemons

one lemon, sliced

one large handful of Italian parsley, chopped

Put a serving platter in a 200° F (100° C) oven to warm.

Using a mallet, thin and stretch out the *scallopine* by pounding down on the centre and working out to the edge of the meat. Avoid punching holes or breaking the *scallopine* into pieces. The *scallopine* should be uniformly as thin as possible with no breaks or holes. The pieces will get larger as you thin them. Slice them in half if necessary to make pieces that will arrange attractively on a plate (about the size of a playing card).

Heat the butter and olive oil together at medium high in a sauté pan large enough to hold four *scallopine* at a time. Dredge four *scallopine* in flour and shake off any excess.

When the butter foam subsides and the butter is just starting to brown, place the floured *scallopine* in the pan so they do not overlap. Brown them quickly on both sides, remove them to a warmed plate, arranging them so that they do not overlap, and sprinkle them lightly with salt. Continue to sauté the remaining *scallopine*, four at a time, dredging them in flour just before putting them in the pan.

When all *scallopine* have been sautéed and removed to a plate, add the lemon juice to the pan and stir a few times to blend the lemon with any remaining juices.

Put the cooked *scallopine* back into the pan four at a time and turn all of the slices over at least once to soak up the lemony juices. Arrange the *scallopine* on the warmed serving platter and garnish with a generous sprinkling of Italian parsley and lemon slices. Serve immediately. **Serving suggestion:** Serve with a lively-flavoured side dish such as *fagiolini verde con peperone e pomodoro*.

Umido di coniglio

RABBIT STEW

serves 4–6

Chicken can be substituted in most of the rabbit or hare (lepre) dishes if you have a hard time finding a source of rabbit meat. If using rabbit, it's important to soak it for a few hours in a salt-water or vinegar brine to mellow the flavour.

one 3–4 lb. (1.5–2 kg) rabbit, cut into serving pieces

2 Tbsp. (30 ml) salt (for soaking the rabbit)

3 Tbsp. (45 ml) butter

2 Tbsp. (30 ml) extra virgin olive oil

1 celery stalk, finely chopped

1 carrot, peeled and finely chopped

1 medium onion, minced

1 1/2 Tbsp. (22 ml) of *pesto di verdure* **or** 1 Tbsp. (15 ml) chopped fresh Italian parsley and 1 tsp. (5 ml) chopped fresh sage

3/4 cup (180 ml) white wine

1 Tbsp. (15 ml) tomato paste

1/2 cup (125 ml) salty dry black olives (optional)

salt and freshly ground pepper to taste

Warm a serving platter in a 200° F (100° C) oven.

Place the rabbit pieces in a deep bowl, cover them with cold water, add 2 Tbsp. (30 ml) of salt and marinate the rabbit for 4 hours. Drain, then rinse the rabbit pieces well with fresh cold water and shake them dry.

Melt the butter and oil at medium high in a sauté pan large enough to hold all of the rabbit pieces. When the butter foam subsides and the butter is just starting to brown, add the rabbit pieces, turn the heat to high and sauté until they are browned on all sides (about 10 minutes). Remove the rabbit to a warmed platter with a slotted spoon.

Lower the heat to medium, add all of the chopped vegetables and the *pesto* or herbs and saute for 8–10 minutes. Add the rabbit pieces back to the pan, blend the white wine and tomato paste together and pour this mixture over the rabbit then toss in the olives (if using).

Gently stir the mixture a few times, then cover and simmer over low heat for about 45 minutes or until the rabbit is tender and cooked through. During the cooking process, turn the rabbit pieces every 15 minutes and check occasionally to ensure there is enough liquid, adding a little water if necessary.

With a slotted spoon, remove the rabbit pieces and olives to a warmed serving platter. Press the pan juices through a sieve placed over a bowl and drizzle the strained juices over the rabbit. Serve hot.

Serving suggestion: serve with grilled *polenta* and a side of *piselli con prosciutto*.

Cosciotto d'agnello arrosto

ROAST LEG OF LAMB

serves 4–6

Lamb from Abruzzo is renowned throughout Italy and is one of the staple meats of Abruzzese cooking. Rosemary, garlic and white wine, found in most lamb recipes from the region, are inserted into slits so that the flavours permeate the meat in this simple-to-prepare roast leg of lamb.

4 garlic cloves, finely chopped

3 tsp. (15 ml) finely chopped fresh rosemary

3 tsp. (15 ml) finely chopped fresh Italian parsley

1/2 cup (125 ml) extra virgin olive oil

3 lb. (1.5 kg) leg of lamb, trimmed of fat and white membrane

salt and freshly ground pepper

1 cup (250 ml) white wine

Preheat oven to 400° F (200° C).

With a mortar and pestle or the back of a spoon, mash together the chopped garlic, rosemary, parsley, a few grindings of black pepper and 2 tsp. (10 ml) of the oil to a *pesto* consistency. Set aside.

Using a sharp knife, cut 8 or 10 deep slits at regular intervals around the leg of lamb. Press a little bit of the garlic-rosemary mixture deep into each slit and press the edges of the slits together to secure the mixture.

Rub the leg of lamb with some of the remaining oil, season with salt and pepper, insert a meat thermometer into the thickest part of the roast and place the roast in an uncovered roasting pan. Drizzle the remaining oil over the lamb and place the pan in the middle r ack of a hot oven.

Roast the lamb for 30 minutes, basting once or twice with the pan juices. After 30 minutes, turn the lamb over, pour the wine over the lamb and roast for a further 25–40 minutes or until the meat thermometer reaches the desired doneness (rare: 125° F/ 52° C; medium rare: 130° F/55° C), basting two or three times with the pan juices during the cooking process.

Remove the lamb to a carving platter and slice it into serving portions. Arrange the slices on a warmed serving platter, strain the pan juices through a sieve and drizzle them over the lamb slices. Serve immediately.

Serving suggestion: Serve with a basic *risotto* or roast potatoes and a side of *zucchini con cipolle e origano*.

Costolette d'abbachio

LAMB CHOPS

serves 4–6

*Oregano, mint and thyme join the lemon juice and zest to create a piquant sauce for these finger-licking baby lamb chops –
a perfect choice for the barbeque season when fresh herbs are readily available.
The chops can also be cooked on a stove-top using a ridged pan.*

2 Tbsp. (30 ml) finely chopped fresh
  oregano

2 Tbsp. (30 ml) finely chopped fresh
  thyme

2 Tbsp. (30 ml) finely chopped fresh
  mint

2 garlic cloves, minced

3 tsp. (15 ml) freshly grated lemon zest

juice from 1/2 lemon

1 tsp.(15 ml) coarse salt

6 Tbsp. (90 ml) extra virgin olive oil

four to six 3/4" (2 cm) thick shoulder-
  blade lamb chops

salt and freshly ground pepper

If using a barbeque, bring the coals to a medium high heat. If cooking on the stovetop, lightly oil a ridged cast iron or grilling pan and heat over high heat until it is hot but not smoking.

To make the sauce, mash the oregano, thyme, mint, garlic, lemon zest, lemon juice, and coarse salt to a paste with a mortar and pestle or the back of a heavy spoon. Transfer the mixture to a bowl and drizzle in the oil, whisking continually until all of the oil is incorporated. Taste and adjust for salt and pepper.

Divide the sauce equally into two bowls – one for basting the lamb, the other for drizzling over the lamb at the end of the cooking process.

Season both sides of the lamb chops with pepper and baste them all over with one of the bowls of sauce.

Grill the lamb chops for four minutes each side (for medium-rare) or for 5 minutes on each side for medium. Baste each side once during the cooking process.

Arrange the chops on a warmed serving platter or individual plates and drizzle the other bowl of sauce over them. Serve immediately.

Serving suggestion: Serve with *Patate al forno con rosmarino* and a side of *peperonata*.

Lombata di maiale con funghi

PORK TENDERLOIN WITH MUSHROOMS

serves 2–4

Pork is a staple in Abruzzese cuisine and is typically used to make cured meats such as mortadella and prosciutto or ground and used in meat sauces and sausages. Uncle Julio developed this tasty tenderloin dish for mushroom lovers. If you cannot find Ortolino, substitute tomato paste or conserva.

1 Tbsp. (15 ml) extra virgin olive oil

1 Tbsp. (15 ml) butter

1 lb. (500 g) pork tenderloin, sliced into 1/2" (1.2 cm) thick slices

1 tsp. (5 ml) *Ortolino* (a tomato/vegetable paste available in most Italian markets) **or** 1 tsp. (5 ml) tomato paste or *conserva*

salt and freshly ground pepper

2 tsp. (10 ml) finely chopped fresh Italian parsley

1/2 tsp. (2 ml) Italian seasoning

1 garlic clove, minced

1/4 lb. (125 g) sliced fresh mushrooms (porcini are best)

1/4 cup (60 ml) beef or chicken broth (if needed)

In a non-stick sauté pan, heat the oil and butter together over medium high heat until the butter foam begins to subside. Brown the tenderloin slices for one minute on each side.

Add the *Ortolino* or tomato paste, a pinch of salt and a few generous grindings of pepper, stir and toss to coat the tenderloin, then cook for 2 minutes more, stirring once or twice. Remove the tenderloin with a slotted spoon to a warm platter.

Add the parsley, Italian seasoning and garlic to the pan, add in the sliced mushrooms, toss to coat the mushrooms in the sauce and sauté for 3–4 minutes, stirring periodically. Add some broth if there are not enough pan juices to cook the mushrooms.

Add the tenderloin slices back in to the pan and toss together with the mushrooms, taste and adjust for salt and pepper and cook for a minute or two until the mushrooms are cooked to taste and the sauce is slightly reduced. Serve immediately.

Serving suggestion: Serve with *piselli con prosciutto* or *fagiolini con peperone e pomodoro*.

Pollo alla cacciatora

HUNTER'S CHICKEN

serves 6

The use of garlic in Nonna's cooking was controversial when her children reached their teenage years. The younger generation did not want to be exuding the scent of garlic as they headed out for the evening. Nonna's compromise was to leave the garlic cloves whole, resulting in a slightly milder garlic flavour in the sauce. Garlic lovers could then spread the succulent cloves on the chicken pieces or bread, while the younger folks, eager to blend with their North American friends, could avoid them altogether. This version of chicken cacciatore uses skinless chicken pieces and lightly flours the chicken breast meat before browning it to prevent it from drying out. If you prefer the skin left on, the meat does not need to be floured before browning.

3 whole chicken breasts, quartered and skinned

8 chicken thighs, boned and skinned

4 Tbsp. (60 ml) flour, seasoned with several grindings of black pepper

4 Tbsp. (60 ml) extra virgin olive oil

1 Tbsp. (15 ml) butter

2 cups (500 ml) finely chopped onions

1 large green pepper, stemmed, seeded and chopped into 1/4" (6 mm) dice

4 large garlic cloves, minced or whole, according to taste

1 cup (250 ml) sliced mushrooms, preferably *porcini*

1 Tbsp. (15 ml) *pesto di verdure* **or** 2 tsp. (10 ml) dried Italian herbs

1 small dried hot chilli pepper, left whole (optional)

4 anchovy filets, finely minced

one 28 oz. (796 ml) tin plum tomatoes, seeded and roughly chopped

salt and freshly ground pepper to taste

1/4 cup (60 ml) Marsala (a sweet fortified wine). If not available, substitute red vermouth or red wine.

Rinse all of the chicken breast and thigh pieces and dry them well.

Put the seasoned flour on a plate, press the skinned breast meat in the flour, shake off any excess flour and set them out on a plate. (This prevents the white meat from drying out during browning. The thigh pieces do not need to be dredged in flour as they are not as prone to drying out.)

In a wide sauté pan large enough to eventually hold all of the chicken, heat the olive oil to medium high. Brown all of the chicken pieces on all sides, 4 or 5 pieces at a time. Remove the browned chicken pieces to a platter and keep them warm while browning the remainder.

Reduce the heat to medium and add the butter to the pan. When the butter foam starts to subside, add the onion, green pepper, garlic, mushrooms, pesto, chilli pepper (if using) and a generous grinding of pepper and sauté everything together for 15 minutes, stirring periodically to prevent burning.

Pollo alla cacciatora

Continued

Put the chicken back in the pan, add the minced anchovies, the chopped tomatoes, and a pinch of salt. Give it a gentle stir to blend all of the ingredients and bring the sauce to bubbling.

Reduce the heat, cover the pan and let it simmer together for 30 minutes, covered, turning the chicken pieces over every 10 minutes and spooning the sauce over them.

After 30 minutes, taste and add salt and pepper to taste, stir in the Marsala and simmer, uncovered, for a further 10 minutes. Remove the chilli pepper (if using).

Preheat the oven to 200° F/100° C. Place a large serving platter in the oven to warm.

When the chicken is in its last 10 minutes of simmering, bring a pot of salted water to a boil and cook the *fettucine* just until *al dente*. Drain the pasta and arrange it on the warmed serving platter.

Spoon the sauce over the pasta and arrange the chicken pieces on top, grate fresh parmigiano generously over all and serve immediately.

Serving suggestion: Serve with a side of *soffritto di spinaci e aglio*, followed by a light *insalata verde*.

Pollo alla cacciatora con olive

CHICKEN AND OLIVES

serves 4–6

This is a popular tomato-less variation on chicken cacciatore in our family. I like to use the salty Moroccan dried black olives. They rehydrate while cooking and turn into plump tasty little nuggets, releasing their salty flavour into the sauce.

3 whole chicken breasts, quartered and skinned

8 chicken thighs, boned and skinned

1/2 cup (125 ml) balsamic vinegar

3 Tbsp. (45 ml) flour seasoned with several grindings of black pepper

1/2 cup (125 ml) extra virgin olive oil

1 medium onion, finely chopped

two slices of *prosciutto*, cut into small dice

1 fresh rosemary sprig **or** 2 tsp. (10 ml) dried rosemary

1 Tbsp. (15 ml) capers

1 pinch chilli pepper flakes

1 cup (250 ml) white wine

1/2 cup (125 ml) chicken stock

1/2 cup (125 ml) dried black salty olives

a few sprigs of fresh rosemary for garnish.

salt and freshly ground pepper

Wash and dry the chicken pieces, then put them in a large bowl, sprinkle the vinegar over them, toss them once or twice to distribute the vinegar and let them marinate for half an hour.

Lift the chicken pieces out of the bowl, shake off any excess moisture and pat them dry with absorbent paper.

Place the seasoned flour in a plate. Press the meat side of each chicken breast piece in the flour, shaking off any excess flour. (This prevents the meat from drying out when it is browned. It is not necessary to flour the thigh pieces as they are not as prone to drying out and too much flour will make the sauce too thick.)

In a sauté pan wide enough to eventually hold all of the chicken pieces, heat the oil to medium high and sauté the chicken pieces 3 or 4 at a time until browned on all sides. Remove the browned chicken pieces with a slotted spoon and set them on a warmed platter while cooking the remaining pieces.

When all chicken pieces have been browned and removed from the pan, sauté the *prosciutto* and onions in the residual oil remaining in the pan on medium heat for 6–8 minutes or until the onions are translucent.

Pollo alla cacciatora con olive

Continued

Add the rosemary, capers and chilli pepper. Mix everything gently together, then add the white wine. Bring the wine to a gentle bubble for 3–4 minutes, then add the chicken stock, stir a few times and add the chicken pieces.

Cover the pan, reduce the heat to a gentle simmer and cook for 15 minutes, turning the chicken pieces over every 5 minutes or so and adding a few tablespoons of water if the sauce is too thick or is drying out.

Add the olives and cook, uncovered, for a final 10–15 minutes or until chicken pieces are cooked through at the thickest part.

Preheat the oven to 200° F/100° C. Place a serving platter in the oven to warm.

When the chicken pieces are cooked through, remove the rosemary sprig and discard it. Lift the chicken pieces and olives onto the warmed serving platter and drizzle the remaining cooking juices over the chicken.

Garnish with fresh rosemary sprigs and serve hot.

Serving suggestion: This chicken can be served over a bed of *fettucine* or is also good with *peperoni imbottiti*.

Pollo arrosto

ROASTED CHICKEN

serves 4

The secret to this succulent chicken of Nonna's is to rotate it periodically as it roasts.
This encases the chicken in a consistently golden and crisp skin and distributes the savoury garlic-and-rosemary flavours
throughout the meat as it cooks. Several chickens can be roasted at a time for larger groups (or delicious leftovers!)

one 3–4 lb. (1.5–2 kg) broiler
  chicken, cleaned,
  trimmed, washed and
  dried

salt and freshly ground
  pepper

3 Tbsp. (45 ml) extra virgin
  olive oil

3 or 4 large garlic cloves

2 tsp. (10 ml) fresh or dried
  rosemary

1 medium carrot, peeled and
  cut in half lengthwise

1 celery stalk, trimmed and
  cut in half lengthwise

several sprigs of fresh
  rosemary for garnish

Preheat the oven to 375° F (190° C). Rub the inside cavities of the chicken generously with salt and pepper. Rub the outside with olive oil and salt and pepper.

Place the garlic cloves, carrot and celery pieces and 1 tsp. (5 ml) of rosemary in the large cavity and skewer or sew the opening closed. Rub the remaining rosemary over the outside.

Place the chicken, breast-up, into a lightly greased roasting pan and into the hot oven. Cook it for 15 minutes in this position. Then turn the chicken over (back-up, breast-down) and cook for 15 minutes in this position. Repeat this rotation every 15 minutes, until the chicken is fully cooked (the leg should move freely when wiggled and the skin should be golden and slightly crispy). Total cooking time will be approximately 1 1/2 hours but will vary depending on the size of the chicken.

Warm a serving platter briefly in the oven. Remove the chicken from the oven to a carving board. Remove and discard the garlic cloves, vegetables and rosemary. Cut the chicken into serving pieces and place them on the warmed serving platter.

Tip the roasting pan and spoon out and discard as much of the fat as possible, reserving any cooking juices. Pour the juices from the carving board back into the roasting pan, add 2 Tbsp. (30 ml) of hot water, taste and adjust for salt and pepper and bring the liquid briefly to a boil over a hot element, whisking to incorporate any tasty bits.

Drizzle the hot juices over the chicken pieces, garnish with fresh rosemary sprigs and serve immediately. **Serving suggestion**: serve with *Peperonata* and roasted or mashed potatoes.

Tacchino di Mama

MY MOTHER'S TURKEY

serves 10-12

My mother has continued Nonna's practice of occasionally preparing turkey in this delicious alternative to the traditional stuffed and roasted variety. The turkey breast is cut into thin scallopine *and prepared separately from the dark meat, which is roasted slowly in a wine-enhanced broth. Delizioso—and no turkey carcass to face at the end of the day! Ask your butcher to cut up the turkey for you to save time and mess.*

one 12–15 lb. (6–8 kg) turkey, divided
    into breast portion, legs, thighs,
    wings, neck, and back

For roasting the dark meat:
turkey legs, thighs, wings and neck
    (freeze the back portion for making a
    future broth)
2 tsp. (10 ml) salt and several grindings
    of black pepper
2 tsp. (10 ml) poultry seasoning
2 garlic cloves, crushed
3 Tbsp. (45 ml) butter
1 cup (250 ml) white wine
1 Tbsp. (15 ml) *pesto di verdure* **or** 2 tsp.
    (10 ml) dried Italian herbs
1 cup (250 ml) chicken broth

To roast the dark meat: preheat the oven to 350° F (180° C). Lightly grease a roasting pan large enough to hold all of the turkey pieces.

Put all of the turkey parts into the prepared roasting pan. Sprinkle it generously with pepper and poultry seasoning and tuck in the garlic cloves. Distribute dabs of butter throughout the turkey parts.

Pour the white wine over the turkey pieces, followed by the *pesto* mixed in the broth. Gently toss the whole mixture to distribute the seasonings and fluids.

Roast the turkey pieces, uncovered, for 2–2 1/2 hours, stirring from time to time and adding salt halfway through the cooking process. The meat is done when it is nicely browned and pulls easily away from the bone.

While the turkey is roasting, prepare the *scallopine* as outlined on the next page.

When roasting is complete, remove the turkey pieces with a slotted spoon to a large heated serving platter. Pour the cooking juices into a measuring cup and skim off and discard the fat. Drizzle some of the juice over the turkey and serve the remaining juice as gravy to be used with the *scallopine* or mashed potatoes.

Continued on next page

Tacchino di Mama

Continued

For the turkey breast scallopine:

1 turkey breast, deboned, sliced across the grain into 1/4" (6 mm) thick *scallopine* and pounded very thin and flat

1/4 cup (60 ml) white wine (**or** 1/2 cup/125 ml if you are using two pans for baking)

1/4 cup (60 ml) chicken broth (**or** 1/2 cup/125 ml if you are using two pans for baking)

1/3 cup (80 ml) grated *parmigiano* cheese

2 cups (500 ml) dried bread crumbs, seasoned with 1/2 tsp. (2 ml) **each** of salt, poultry seasoning and garlic powder

2 eggs, lightly beaten and placed in a wide bowl

1/2 cup (125 ml) safflower or vegetable oil

2 lemons, sliced

To prepare the scallopine: mix the grated cheese with the seasoned bread crumbs in a bowl. Set out the bowl of beaten eggs and the bowl of bread crumb/cheese mixture on your work surface.

One by one, dip a turkey *scallopine* in the egg and coat it thoroughly, gently shake off any excess egg, then dredge the *scallopine* in the seasoned bread crumb/cheese mixture. Shake off any excess crumbs and lay the scallopine out on a platter for a few minutes to allow the two coatings to marry.

When all of the *scallopine* have been coated, heat the oil to medium high in a large sauté pan. When the oil is hot, begin sautéing the *scallopine* 3 or 4 at a time on both sides, just until the coating turns crispy and a honey golden colour.

Pour 1/4 cup (60 ml) each of wine and broth into the bottom of a lightly buttered baking or roasting pan large enough to eventually hold all of the *scallopine* in one layer (or use two pans with 1/4 cup/60 ml each of wine and broth in each pan).

Lay the sautéed *scallopine* on top of the broth/wine mixture in the prepared baking pan. Bake the *scallopine* for 30 to 35 minutes in a 350° F (180° C) oven, turning them once during the baking process.

If your oven cannot accommodate the *scallopine* pans and the dark meat roasting pan at the same time, put the *scallopine* pans in after the dark meat has finished roasting. Cover the roasted dark meat and keep it warm while the *scallopine* are baking.

After baking, remove the *scallopine* to a heated serving platter, scatter lemon slices over them and serve them with the roasted dark meat.

Serving suggestion: This turkey is good served with all of the usual trimmings which accompany roast turkey, such as mashed potatoes and steamed or roasted brussel sprouts.

Frittata con zucchini
ITALIAN OMELETTE WITH ZUCCHINI

serves 4

As an alternative to meat, Nonna had a variety of egg dishes which she served on Fridays.
The versatility of frittata *made it a favourite choice.*
The basic process for making a frittata *can be followed for almost any combination of ingredients.*
The frittata *is prepared in three steps. First, the featured ingredients, such as sautéed vegetables, are prepared.*
Next, in a separate bowl, the eggs are beaten and then mixed with the cheese. Finally, the featured ingredients are mixed with
the eggs and cheese and cooked slowly together in a buttered pan, and finished briefly under a hot broiler to firm up the top.

3 cups (750 ml) unpeeled thinly sliced small zucchini

1 Tbsp. 15 ml) salt

5 Tbsp. (75 ml) butter

1 medium onion, very thinly sliced

2 Tbsp. (30 ml) finely chopped fresh Italian parsley

1 Tbsp. (15 ml) finely chopped fresh thyme

2 garlic cloves, minced

salt and freshly ground pepper

6 large eggs

1/3 cup plus 2 Tbsp. (110 ml) freshly shredded *fontina* or *asiago* cheese

Put the zucchini slices into a colander set over a bowl, salt them liberally, toss to distribute the salt and allow them to sit for 20 minutes. This process will extract soome of the moisture from the zucchini and prevent them from getting mushy when sautéed. After 20 minutes, rinse the zucchini well under cold water, drain them and rinse and drain a second time. Dry them by shaking them gently in a towel or absorbent paper.

In a large sauté pan, saute the onions and 3 Tbsp. (45 ml) of the butter on medium heat for 6–8 minutes. Add the drained zucchini, parsley, thyme, garlic and a generous grinding of pepper and sauté for 10–12 minutes or until the zucchini are softened and lightly browned on both sides and the onions are carmelized. Remove the vegetables with a slotted spoon, drain well and allow to cool for a few minutes. Wipe the residual cooking butter from the pan with absorbent paper.

In a mixing bowl, beat the eggs, a pinch of salt and several grindings of fresh pepper until the whites and yolks are well blended. Mix in 1/3 cup of the cheese and all of the drained zucchini mixture.

Melt the remaining 2 Tbsp. (30 ml) butter over low heat in the sauté pan, then add the egg and zucchini mixture and cook over low heat for 12-15 minutes until the eggs have set and the bottom is lightly golden.

Sprinkle the remaining cheese over the top of the *frittata* and place the pan under the broiler for a minute or so, just until the surface is firm and the cheese is melted. **Serving suggestion**: Serve with *Peperonata* and *Patate al forno con rosmarino*.

Frittata con peperoni misti
ITALIAN OMELETTE WITH MIXED PEPPERS

serves 4

This is one of my favourite combinations, in taste, texture and appearance.
The peppers create a happy jumble of colours against the bright yellow palette of eggs. As a decadent treat, we sometimes
put a few slices of gorgonzola or cambozola cheese on top before putting the frittata under the broiler. Squisito!

4 Tbsp. (60 ml) extra virgin olive oil

1 medium onion, finely chopped

1 garlic clove, minced

1 medium red pepper, seeded and sliced into 1/4" (6 mm) strips

1 medium yellow pepper, seeded and sliced into 1/4" (6 mm) strips

1 medium orange pepper, seeded and sliced into 1/4" (6 mm) strips

1 Tbsp. (15 ml) fresh basil, chopped or 1 tsp. (5 ml) dried basil

salt and freshly ground pepper

2 Tbsp. (30 ml) butter

6 or 7 eggs (depending on the size of the peppers)

1/3 cup (80 ml) freshly grated parmigiano cheese

1 oz. (30 g) *gorgonzola* or *cambozola* cheese (optional)

In a large sauté pan, sauté the oil and onions on medium heat for 6–8 minutes. Add the garlic and sauté for a further 2–3 minutes.

Add the sliced peppers, basil, a pinch of salt and a few grindings of pepper to the pan, turn the heat to medium low and sauté, uncovered, for 18–20 minutes, stirring periodically, until the peppers are tender but not mushy.

Remove the pan from the heat, move the sautéed mixture to one side of the pan and tip the pan so that any residual oil drains out of the pepper mixture and pools on the opposite side of the pan. Remove the sautéed mixture with a slotted spoon and reserve. Discard any residual cooking oil.

In a mixing bowl, beat 6 of the eggs, a pinch of salt and a few grindings of pepper until the whites and yolks are well blended. Mix in the *parmigiano* and the sautéed pepper mixture. If the mixture needs more liquid, add another beaten egg.

Melt the butter in the sauté pan, add the egg and sautéed pepper mixture and cook over very low heat for 12–15 minutes until the eggs have set and the bottom is lightly golden.

Place the pan under the broiler for a minute or so, just until the surface is firm. If desired, place thin strips of the *gorgonzola* cheese on top of the *frittata* before putting it under the broiler. Serve the *frittata* hot.

Serving suggestion: This *frittata* pairs well with an *insalata di ceci e prezzemolo* or a *soffritto di spinaci e aglio*.

Uovi affogati

EGGS POACHED IN SAUCE

serves 4–6

"Affogare" means to poach.
Instead of water, the eggs are poached in a tomato-onion sauce in this easy-to-prepare brunch dish.
Peperonata can also be substituted for the onions and tomato sauce.

3 Tbsp. (45 ml) butter

1 Tbsp. (15 ml) extra virgin olive oil

2 medium onions, very thinly sliced

1 garlic clove, minced

2 cups (500 ml) Basic tomato sauce

6 large eggs

1/2 cup. (125 ml) freshly grated
   parmigiano

6 slices Italian bread, toasted and
   brushed with olive oil

fresh Italian parsley for garnish

Melt the butter and oil over a medium heat in a large sauté pan with a lid. When the butter foam starts to subside, add the onions, and sauté at medium-low heat for 10 minutes, then add the garlic and cook for a further 3–4 minutes or until the garlic and onions are golden and soft.

Add the tomato sauce, increase the heat to medium and cook at a gentle bubble for 4 or 5 minutes. Break the eggs into the tomato mixture at regular intervals and cook them for about 1 minute.

Spoon a tablespoon (15 ml) of *parmigiano* cheese over each egg, cover the pan and reduce the heat. Simmer for 3 or 4 minutes until the eggs are firm and the cheese is melted.

Place toasted bread slices on a warm serving platter, lift an egg onto each slice of bread and spoon sauce around the toast. Garnish with fresh parsley and a few grindings of black pepper and serve immediately.

Serving suggestion: Serve with a side of *Patate al forno con rosmarino* or *patate con peperone* for brunch or a simple dinner.

Dandelion revisited

The importance of vegetables in the Abruzzese diet is reflected in the variety of vegetable dishes served alongside the meat or fish course and the salad which invariably follows. Just as most of Nonna's meals started with soup, the last course before dessert was usually a fresh salad of seasonal greens tossed with a simple oil and wine vinegar dressing. Fresh greens were available throughout most of the year; in the warm months, the *giardino* produced our daily bowl of red and green lettuce or young *radicchio* leaves. When the weather cooled, our salads were made from the waxy, slightly bitter leaves of the heartier varieties of *radicchio*, cultivated and protected in the cellar under gunny sacks to prevent freezing.

One of the most memorable salads was the one we made in the late spring when the new dandelion was sprouting. Dandelion, or *dens lionis* (meaning lion's teeth because of the jagged, teeth-like shape of the leaves) has, unfortunately, acquired a reputation as a reviled weed against which war is regularly waged in North American lawns and gardens. However, if picked at just the right moment, when the new leaves are bright, almost-lime green and silky and the flower buds are still tight little buttons, dandelion is a delicious edible green, served raw in salads or sandwiches or steamed and sautéed in olive oil with onions. One of our happiest childhood adventures was going out into the woods, with the adults, to collect the little dandelion plants in a big bag. When we got home, we helped to wash them, carefully cleaning the delicate little flower bulbs so they stayed intact when the salad was tossed.

It goes without saying that dandelion for eating should not be harvested from lawns or fields which have been chemically treated.

Papa Vincenzo and Nonna Sofia with fresh bounty from the woods.

Salad and vegetable recipes

Wild dandelion salad

serves 4–6

A bowlful of freshly-picked dandelion plants with flower buds (not yet opened)

2 hard-boiled eggs

5 or 6 anchovies (optional)

2–3 Tbsp. (30–45 ml) good quality red wine vinegar

3–4 Tbsp. (45–60 ml) extra virgin olive oil

salt and freshly ground pepper

Break off the long root threads of the dandelion plants and pull the leaves from their base. (For very small plants, just break off the root threads but leave the whole plant intact, unopened flowers and all.)

Place the dandelion to soak in a bowl of cold water and wash each leaf, small plant and flower bud carefully, making sure to remove any dirt which might be trapped where the leaves attach to the root. Rinse, and soak them a second time. Shake the dandelion dry in a colander lined with a towel to absorb extra moisture.

Arrange the dandelion in a salad bowl. Break the anchovies into 1/2" (12 mm) pieces into the bowl and toss them to distribute. Thinly slice the hard-boiled eggs and distribute the slices over the salad.

Drizzle the olive oil over the salad and toss it gently to distribute and coat the leaves. Drizzle the red wine vinegar over the salad, add a good sprinkle of salt and 7 or 8 grindings of freshly-ground pepper and toss to distribute. Taste for seasonings and adjust as necessary. Enjoy at once.

Sautéed dandelion

serves 4–6

*A favourite meatless meal on Friday during dandelion season
was a bowl of asparagi con riso soup followed by pan-fried dandelion
with slices of hard-boiled egg and homemade bread.*

6 to 8 cups (500 g) dandelion leaves,
    well cleaned and separated
1 small onion, finely chopped
1 large garlic clove, minced
3 Tbsp. (45 ml) extra virgin olive oil
salt and freshly ground pepper to taste
red wine vinegar (optional)

Bring to a boil 1" (2.5 cm) of salted water in a pot large enough to hold the dandelion.

Add the dandelion, shake the pot to distribute and steam, covered, for several minutes until the dandelion leaves are thoroughly wilted. Drain the dandelion well, chop it roughly and set it aside.

In a heavy sauté pan, sauté the onion and garlic and a few grindings of pepper in olive oil until the onion is soft and lightly golden (8–10 minutes). Add the cooked dandelion to the pan and sauté together for 3 or 4 minutes, stirring it periodically.

    Serve it hot with a generous grinding of pepper or warm with a drizzle of red wine vinegar.

Insalata di ceci e prezzemolo

CHICK PEAS AND PARSLEY SALAD

serves 4

The wide-leafed Italian parsley has a more intense flavour and a silkier texture than the curly leafed variety. It complements the comparatively bland taste of the ceci in this salad which was a regular on Nonna's table.

3 to 4 Tbsp. (45 to 60 ml) white wine vinegar

4 Tbsp. (60 ml) extra virgin olive oil

salt and freshly ground pepper

one 19 oz. (796 ml) tin chickpeas, drained

1/2 cup (125 ml) chopped fresh Italian parsley leaves

10 or 12 small chives, chopped

3 spring onions, green stems removed and white bulbs thinly sliced (**or** use 2 small shallot bulbs if spring onions are not available)

Pour 3 Tbsp. (45 ml) of the vinegar into a small bowl, then slowly drizzle in the oil, whisking constantly until the mixture blends and the oil and vinegar do not separate. Whisk in a pinch of salt and several grindings of black pepper. Set aside.

In a separate bowl, toss the chickpeas, parsley, chives, and sliced onions. Drizzle the oil and vinegar mixture over, toss, then taste and adjust for vinegar, salt and pepper.

Let the salad rest for an hour or so at room temperature, tossing periodically. Add more vinegar to taste. Serve at room temperature.

Insalata di asparagi

ASPARAGUS SALAD

serves 4–6

When the asparagus spears are sprouting,
this is an easy and tasty way to enjoy their delicate taste.

5 Tbsp. (75 ml) extra virgin olive oil

3 Tbsp. (45 ml) white wine vinegar

2 Tbsp. (30 ml) chopped fresh Italian parsley

salt and freshly ground pepper

20–24 fresh asparagus spears, washed and wooden part of stem removed

1 spring onion bulb, white part only, finely sliced **or** 1 shallot bulb, peeled and finely sliced

one or two fresh parsley sprigs for garnish

Put the vinegar in a small bowl and gradually drizzle in the olive oil, whisking constantly, so the oil and vinegar blend and emulsify slightly. Mix in the parsley, a pinch of salt and a few grindings of pepper and set the mixture aside.

Bring 1" (2.5 cm) of salted water to a boil in a large pot, or 2" (5 cm) in an asparagus steamer. Add the asparagus spears, cover and steam them for about 6–8 minutes (depending on the thickness of the asparagus) just until they are tender-crisp but not soft.

Remove the asparagus from the hot water, drain them well and place them on a serving platter. Top them with the sliced onion or shallot and drizzle the oil and vinegar dressing over all.

Allow the asparagus and onions to sit at room temperature for an hour or so to absorb the dressing. Garnish with fresh parsley sprigs and serve at room temperature.

Insalata verde

GREEN SALAD

serves 4–6

After the meat or fish course, every meal was punctuated with a salad.
The most typical salad was an insalata verde, fresh greens tossed in an oil and vinegar at the table just before serving.

When the weather got too cold for the radicchio plants to remain outdoors, they were transplanted to sand-filled boxes in the cellar so that salad greens would be available throughout the winter. The winter radicchio leaves are waxier and more bitter than their younger spring and summer versions—an acquired taste.
Some prefer them steamed and sautéed and finished with a sprinkling of vinegar.

one small head of radicchio **or**
   3 generous handfuls of young
   radicchio leaves
one large head of leafy endive or
   romaine lettuce
4 Tbsp. (60 ml) extra virgin olive oil
2–3 Tbsp. (30–45 ml) good quality
   balsamic or red wine vinegar
salt and freshly ground black pepper

Separate the *radicchio* leaves and lettuce leaves and soak, clean and dry them well.

Tear the leaves into bite-sized pieces into the salad bowl. Cover it with a damp cloth and keep it cool until ready to serve.

When ready to serve, drizzle the oil over the greens and toss, then add the vinegar, a generous sprinkle of salt, and several grindings of fresh pepper and gently toss a few times.

Taste and adjust for vinegar and seasoning and serve immediately.

Fagiolini verde con peperone e pomodoro

GREEN BEANS WITH PEPPERS AND TOMATOES

serves 4–6

Uncle Julio warns that only the freshest of green beans are permissible for this favourite dish
inspired by Nonna's method of pan cooking the beans in tomato sauce.
If you are lucky enough to have leftovers, they are delicious served on toasted Italian bread for lunch.

4 Tbsp. (60 ml) extra virgin olive oil

1 medium onion, thinly sliced

1 large green pepper, seeded and sliced into 1" (2.5 cm) wide strips

2 large ripe tomatoes, skinned, seeded and chopped

1 lb. (500 g) green beans, washed and ends snapped or sliced off

2/3 cup (160 ml) water, approximately

salt and freshly ground pepper to taste

Heat the oil and onions in a heavy pan or skillet and sauté the onions at medium heat for 6–8 minutes or until they are soft and translucent.

Add the green pepper strips, chopped tomatoes and a pinch of salt and cook, uncovered, at a high simmer, stirring occasionally to prevent burning, until the tomatoes start to take on the appearance of a sauce (about 25–30 minutes).

Add the green beans and stir to coat the beans with the sauce. Add 1/3 cup of the water, several generous grindings of pepper and salt to taste and simmer, stirring periodically, for 30–40 minutes.

Halfway through the cooking process, taste and correct for salt and pepper, and add a tablespoon or two (15–30 ml) of water if the sauce is drying out too much before the beans are fully cooked.

The dish is ready when the beans and peppers are very tender, and most of the fluids have cooked off, leaving a thick, almost tomato-paste-like sauce coating the beans. Serve hot.

Zucchini and flower fritters

serves 4–6

Nonna always used young zucchini before they got too large so that they would hold their shape and not become mushy when cooked. Finding one of the wonderful little frittered flowers among the zucchini was a highly sought-after prize among the young diners.

8–10 zucchini flowers, not yet opened

3 or 4 fresh, young zucchini, about 2–3" (5–7.5 cm) in diameter

salt

1/2 cup (125 ml) flour, seasoned with pepper

4 eggs

4 Tbsp. (60 ml) *parmigiano* or *romano* cheese

4–5" (10–13 cm) of safflower or vegetable oil in a medium-sized heavy sauce pan or deep fryer

Wash the flowers, shake out any water and dry them very well. Gently scrub the skin of the zucchini until smooth, cut off and discard the ends and slice the zucchini into 1/4" (6mm) thin rounds.

Salt the zucchini slices liberally, put them in a colander over a large bowl and let them sit for a half hour. This drains some of the water from the zucchini and prevents the fritters from being soggy. Rinse the slices well in cold water and drain them well, then pat them dry after draining.

Dredge the zucchini slices and the flowers in the flour, shake off any excess flour and lay them out on a rack so they aren't touching.

In a medium bowl, whisk the eggs, add the cheese, a pinch of salt and a few grindings of pepper and whisk again until well-blended.

Heat the oil to hot but not smoking. Using a fork, dip the zucchini slices and the flowers one by one into the egg and cheese mixture and coat them well. Place the dipped zucchini slices and flowers, 3 or 4 at a time, into the hot oil.

Fry them until golden brown and crispy, turning once in the frying process. (Be careful – the oil may splatter.) Place the fried slices and flowers on a clean cloth or paper towels to soak up any excess oil and sprinkle with salt. Serve hot.

Pomodori imbottiti

STUFFED TOMATOES

serves 4

This is a delicious way to enjoy the fresh tomato harvest.

6 medium-sized firm ripe tomatoes

salt and freshly ground pepper

1 cup (250 ml) coarse dried bread crumbs

5 Tbsp. (75 ml) *romano* or *pecorino* cheese

4 Tbsp. (60 ml) finely chopped fresh Italian parsley

1 tsp. (5 ml) *pesto di basilico* **or** 2 tsp. (10 ml) chopped fresh basil

1 garlic clove, crushed and minced

1/3 cup (80 ml) chicken broth or water

6 thin slices *pancetta* or bacon

salt and freshly ground pepper

Heat the oven to 350° F (180° C)

Carve a 1" (2.5 cm) circle around the stem of each tomato with a sharp knife and remove the stem and a cone of the pulp extending into the centre of the tomato. With a small spoon, remove the seeds. This creates the well for the stuffing. Lightly salt and pepper the interior of the tomatoes.

In a bowl, combine the bread crumbs, grated cheese, parsley, *pesto*, garlic, a sprinkle of salt and a few grindings of pepper and the broth or water.

Stuff each tomato with a quarter of this mixture—it should mound up a little over the well. Lay a strip of *pancetta* or bacon over each tomato, place the tomatoes upright in a buttered baking dish and bake them for 15–20 minutes, or until *pancetta* or bacon is crisp and the stuffing is golden brown. Serve hot.

Peperoni imbottiti

STUFFED PEPPERS

serves 4

*When the plump green peppers were ready to be picked, much of the harvest was used in preserves
such as* stuffatello *and* antipasto *for use in the winter months. However, some were always saved for eating fresh
in this easy and delicious dish which is a good way to use extra cooked rice and meat.*

4 medium-sized firm green peppers,
   well washed

salt and freshly ground pepper

1 Tbsp. (15 ml) extra virgin olive oil

6 Tbsp. (90 ml) grated *romano* or
   parmigiano cheese

4 Tbsp. (60 ml) fresh Italian parsley,
   chopped

2 tsp. (10 ml) *pesto di basilica* **or**
   4 tsp. (20 ml) chopped fresh basil

6 filets anchovies, finely minced

1 medium onion, minced

3 cups (750 ml) cooked rice (brown or
   white; long-grained or short-grained)

1 cup (250 ml) cooked chicken, veal, beef
   or lamb, finely minced

2 eggs, lightly beaten

salt and freshly ground pepper

extra virgin olive oil

1/3 cup (80 ml) water

2 Tbsp. (30 ml) *conserva* or tomato
   paste, dissolved in 1 cup (250 ml)
   hot chicken broth or hot water

Preheat oven to 375°F (190° C)

Cut a circle around the stem of each green pepper and carefully remove the
stem and seeds and white core. Reserve the stem circles to serve as "lids"
during the cooking process.

To lightly steam the peppers before baking, place 1" (2.5 cm) of water
in a pot large enough to hold all of the peppers and arrange a steaming
basket over the water. Arrange the peppers, stem end up, in the steaming
basket, bring the water to a boil, cover and steam for 3 minutes. Remove the
lid, turn the peppers over, cover the pot and steam for a further 3 minutes.
Check for readiness—the pepper flesh should be parcooked but still
somewhat firm.

Remove the peppers from the pot, shake off any moisture, lightly salt
and pepper the interiors of the peppers, drizzle in a little bit of olive oil,
rub the outside wall with olive oil and let them cool while you are
assembling the filling.

In a mixing bowl, combine thoroughly the cheese, parsley, *pesto*, anchovies,
onion, rice, meat, eggs, a pinch of salt and a few grindings of pepper.

Using a spoon small enough to fit into the opening on the peppers, stuff
each pepper with an equal portion of this mixture and place the stuffed

peppers upright in a buttered baking dish. (If the peppers do not stand up straight, slice off the points on the bottom to make them sit flat.)

Place a stem cover over each pepper and arrange them, stuffing end up, in a well-greased ribbed roasting pan or on a rack in a baking pan. Pour 1/3 cup of water into the bottom of the pan and bake the stuffed peppers in a hot oven for 20 minutes.

Pull the pan out of the oven temporarily, remove and discard the stem caps and drizzle the tomato paste mixture evenly over the partially baked peppers.

Continue to bake the peppers for a further 20 minutes or until they are tender when pierced with a fork. Serve hot.

Peperonata

PEPPERS AND TOMATO

serves 4

Peperonata can be served as a vegetable dish, used in frittata
or tossed with linguine *or* fettucine *for a light, meatless pasta.*

6 Tbsp. (90 ml) extra virgin olive oil

1 large onion, chopped into a medium
dice

2 garlic cloves, crushed and finely
chopped

4 large red peppers, cored, seeded and
cut lengthwise into 1/4" (6 mm)
strips

3 large yellow peppers, cored, seeded,
and cut lengthwise into 1/4" (6 mm)
strips

1 lb. (500 g) ripe plum tomatoes,
skinned, seeded and coarsely
chopped

salt and freshly ground black pepper

2 Tbsp. (30 ml) capers, drained

a generous handful of basil leaves,
coarsely torn

Heat 4 Tbsp. (60 ml) of the oil and the onions in a heavy sauté pan large enough to hold all of the ingredients. Sauté the onions for 6–8 minutes, add the garlic and sauté for a further 2–3 minutes until the onions and garlic are translucent and soft.

Add the peppers to the pan and sauté, uncovered, over a medium heat for about 15 minutes, tossing occasionally to distribute the heat and prevent burning, until the peppers are tender but not mushy.

Add the tomatoes, season with salt and a few grindings of pepper and cook, uncovered, for a further 15–20 minutes, stirring occasionally.

Remove the pan from the heat and cool the mixture to lukewarm, then stir in the remaining olive oil, the capers and the basil.

Serve at room temperature.

MIXED PEPPERS

serves 4

The bright colours of peppers are vividly captured in this mouth-watering combination.
Try it in a frittata or over grilled polenta slices.

4 Tbsp. (60 ml) extra virgin olive oil
1 medium onion, finely chopped
1 garlic clove, minced
1 red pepper, seeded and sliced into
    1/4" (6 mm) strips
1 yellow pepper, seeded and sliced into
    1/4" (6 mm) strips
1 orange pepper, seeded and sliced into
    1/4" (6 mm) strips
salt and freshly ground pepper
1 Tbsp. (15 ml) fresh basil, chopped **or**
    1 tsp. (5 ml) dried basil
fresh Italian parsley, for garnish

In a large sauté pan, sauté the oil and onions on medium heat for 6–8 minutes. Add the garlic and sauté for a further 2–3 minutes.

Add the sliced peppers, a pinch of salt, a few generous grindings of pepper and the basil, turn the heat to medium low and sauté for 18–20 minutes until the peppers are tender but not mushy.

Remove the pan from the heat, move the sautéed mixture to one side of the pan and tip the pan so that the oil drains out of the pepper mixture and pools on the opposite side of the pan. Discard the drained oil (or use it for sautéing meat or a *soffritto* if you are cooking several dishes. It has a delicious flavour.)

Remove the drained pepper mixture with a slotted spoon to a warmed serving platter and serve hot, garnished with parsley.

Soffritto di spinaci e aglio
SAUTÉED SPINACH AND GARLIC

serves 3-4

This method can also be used with beet greens or Swiss chard.

2 cups (500 ml) water, well-salted

1 lb. (500 g) fresh spinach, cleaned and washed and stems trimmed

3 Tbsp. (45 ml) extra virgin olive oil

4 large garlic cloves, crushed and minced

salt and freshly ground pepper

2 Tbsp. (30 ml) red wine or balsamic vinegar (optional)

Bring salted water to a boil in a saucepan large enough to hold the spinach. Put in the spinach, cover and cook for 3–4 minutes, shaking the pot once or twice to distribute the leaves as they wilt.

When the spinach is completely wilted and has turned a deep green, remove it from the heat and drain it well. Roughly chop the drained spinach and set it aside.

Heat the olive oil and garlic in a large sauté pan. Sauté the garlic in oil for 3–4 minutes or until soft and lightly coloured. Put in the spinach, add a generous grinding of pepper and toss to distribute the oil and garlic.

Sauté for 4–5 minutes, mixing frequently to prevent sticking. Taste and correct for salt and pepper seasoning.

Serve the spinach hot or at room temperature with a little drizzle of red wine or balsamic vinegar.

Zucchini con cipolle e origano
ZUCCHINI WITH ONIONS AND OREGANO

serves 4-6

This dish is best when made with small, firm zucchini which don't get mushy when cooked.
It is a mildly flavoured side dish which pairs well with intensely flavoured main courses, such as pollo con olive.

1 1/2 lb. (750 g) small-to-medium
zucchini, scrubbed well and
ends removed

3 Tbsp. (45 ml) butter

3 small or 1 large onion, sliced
    very thin

2 tsp. (10 ml) fresh oregano, finely cut
    or 1 tsp. (5 ml) dried oregano

salt and freshly ground pepper

balsamic vinegar (optional)

Slice the zucchini uniformly into thin slices. Salt the slices liberally and let them sit in a colander over a bowl for about 1/2 hour to draw out extra moisture. Rinse the zucchini slices very thoroughly, drain them well, rinse and drain them a second time. Put them in a clean tea towel and gently shake them to dry.

Put the onion and butter in a wide sauté pan (so there is lots of room to spread the zucchini when you add them later). Cook the butter and onion over medium heat for 8–10 minutes or until the onions soften and turn golden.

Add the sliced zucchini, the oregano and several grindings of pepper and turn the heat to medium high. Sauté uncovered, carefully turning the zucchini slices after several minutes so the zucchini are uniformly cooked and the onion doesn't burn. The zucchini are done when they turn a golden brown at the edges and are tender, not mushy. (The cooking time will vary depending on the age, size and thickness of the zucchini.)

Adjust for seasoning, add a drizzle of balsamic vinegar if desired and serve hot or warm.

Asparagi al forno
BAKED ASPARAGUS

serves 6

These asparagus can be prepared ahead up to the point of baking and served either as an antipasto *(appetizer)*
or a side dish with a meat or fish course. The asparagus are par-cooked and then wrapped up along with some soft pecorino
or fontina *cheese into single servings, secured with a piece of* prosciutto *or roasted red peppers (for a vegetarian alternative)*
and baked. This same technique works well with fresh green beans.

24 fresh medium thick asparagus spears, washed and woody ends broken off

6 thin slices of *prosciutto* **or** 1 roasted red pepper, sliced into 1/2" (1.2 cm) strips

1 Tbsp. (15 ml) extra virgin olive oil

1/3 lb. (185 g) soft *pecorino* or *fontina* cheese, grated

Half fill a large bowl with cold water and set it aside.

Bring 2" (5 cm) of water to boil in a pot wide enough to accommodate the asparagus horizontally. Immerse the asparagus in the boiling water (you may need to do them in two batches), bring the water back to a boil, cover the pot and cook for 3–4 minutes (less time for thinner asparagus).

Check for texture; the asparagus should be tender but still crunchy. Lift the asparagus from the water with a slotted spoon and plunge them into the bowl of cold water to arrest the cooking process.

Preheat the oven to 400° F (200° C). Lightly grease a casserole dish large enough to hold all of the asparagus.

Lay the 6 *prosciutto* slices or roasted red pepper strips out flat on a work surface. Drain the cooled asparagus well, then lay 4 of them across the centre of each *prosciutto* or red pepper strip.

Brush the asparagus lightly with olive oil, then wrap the *prosciutto* or red pepper over and around the asparagus to secure the bundle. Arrange the bundles in a buttered baking dish and sprinkle 1/6 of the grated cheese over each bundle.

Bake the bundles in a preheated oven for 15 minutes or until the cheese is melted and starting to turn golden. Serve immediately.

Freshly grated mozzarella, pecorino and fontina cheeses are lined up in preparation for the lasagna assembly line—Valerie Mitchell, Fran Pardee, Lori LaRose-Guest, and Lorraine Sovran Taylor.

Cheese is used liberally in Abruzzese cooking, in soups and vegetable dishes, as well as with pasta.

(See La Cucina Abruzzese, page 8, and Formaggio, page 144.)

Dallas and Nonno Julio lift a pan of Pollo arrosto *from the oven.*

The process of turning the chickens periodically as they roast produces a deep golden colour and tender succulent meat.

(See Pollo Arrosto, page 76)

Patate al forno con rosmarino

OVEN-ROASTED ROSEMARY POTATOES

serves 4 6

These potatoes smell wonderful as they bake with the rosemary.

6 medium potatoes, washed, peeled and cut into 1" (2.5 cm) cubes

4 Tbsp. (60 ml) extra virgin olive oil

1 Tbsp. butter

1 large sprig of fresh rosemary, separated into small bunches and main stem discarded

salt and freshly ground pepper

Soak the potato cubes in a large bowl of cold, well-salted water for 1/2 hour. Drain well, rinse and drain well again.

Heat the oven to 350° F (180° C).

Toss the potatoes in the olive oil, ensuring they are well coated. Add a few generous grindings of pepper. Put the potatoes in a greased heavy roasting pan or casserole dish large enough to hold the potatoes in one layer.

Distribute the butter in small dabs throughout the potatoes and tuck in bunches of rosemary.

Bake the potatoes for about one hour, gently tossing them every 10–15 minutes to prevent sticking.

Test at 45 minutes and remove or continue baking as necessary until the pieces are cooked through but retain their shape. Remove and discard any large rosemary pieces before serving. Serve hot.

Patate con peperoni

POTATOES AND PEPPERS

serves 6

This potato, onion and pepper bake is a tasty alternative to roasted potatoes and goes well with lamb.

6 medium-size russet potatoes (do not use new potatoes), peeled and cut into 8–10 wedges

2/3 cup (160 ml) bread crumbs

2/3 cup (160 ml) freshly grated *parmigiano* cheese

2 Tbsp. (30 ml) melted butter

1/3 cup (80 ml) extra virgin olive oil

2 medium green peppers, stemmed, seeded and sliced into 1/2" (12 mm) strips

1 small onion, thinly sliced and separated into rings

5 or 6 large garlic cloves, lightly crushed

1 Tbsp. (15 ml) fresh rosemary

salt and freshly ground pepper

Preheat the oven to 375° F (190° C).

Soak the potato slices in a bowl of well-salted cold water for half an hour, then drain them, rinse them, drain them again and set aside.

Mix the bread crumbs, *parmigiano* cheese and melted butter together and set aside.

Distribute the oil over the bottom of a casserole dish or heavy roasting pan large enough to accommodate all of the ingredients in one layer.

Add the potato wedges, green peppers*, thinly sliced onion, garlic cloves and rosemary to the pan, sprinkle generously with salt and several grindings of pepper, toss to coat with oil and distribute the mixture evenly in the dish. (*If you prefer a crunchier green pepper, add them halfway through the cooking process instead).

Sprinkle the bread crumb-cheese-butter mixture over all and toss again.

Bake, uncovered, in the hot oven until the potatoes are cooked through but not mushy (approximately 45–50 minutes), stirring and scraping the bottom with a lifter 2 or 3 times during the cooking process to prevent sticking.

Taste and adjust for salt and pepper. Serve hot.

Piselli con prosciutto

PEAS WITH PROSCIUTTO

serves 4

The saltiness of the prosciutto *brings out the sweetness of the peas in this easy to prepare dish.*

2 Tbsp. (30 ml) butter

1 small onion, minced

4 cups (1 l) fresh shelled or frozen peas, defrosted

1/2 cup (125 ml) chicken stock (if using fresh peas)

salt and freshly ground pepper

1/4 lb. (125 g) thinly sliced *prosciutto*, torn into bite-sized pieces

Put the butter and onion in a sauté pan, heat to medium and sauté for 6–8 minutes, until the onion is translucent.

Add the fresh peas and the chicken stock (or the frozen peas and no stock), toss and cook them gently until tender (about 5 minutes).

Add the *prosciutto* and sauté for a further minute or so. Add a grinding of black pepper and serve hot.

Carciofi imbottiti

STUFFED ARTICHOKES

serves 4

When fresh artichokes are available, this savoury stuffed version is a satisfying way to enjoy them.

For the stuffing:

6 *pancetta* slices, 1/4" (6 mm) thick

2 cups (500 ml) dried Italian bread crumbs

1/2 cup (125 ml) finely grated *parmigiano* cheese

3 garlic cloves, minced

1/4 cup (60 ml) finely chopped fresh
   Italian parsley

salt and freshly ground pepper

2 Tbsp. (30 ml) chicken or beef broth

1/4 cup (60 ml) extra virgin olive oil

1/4 lb. (125 g) *fontina* cheese, grated

For the artichokes:

4 fresh artichokes (look for ones with
   firmly packed healthy leaves)

juice from 1/2 lemon

2 cups (500 ml) water

1/2 cup (125 ml) dry white wine

1/4 cup (60 ml) extra virgin olive oil

1 bay leaf

1/2 lemon, sliced

1 garlic clove, crushed

1/2 tsp. (2 ml) salt

10 whole black peppercorns

To make the stuffing, slice the *pancetta* into a small dice and sauté the *pancetta* pieces over medium heat until well browned. Remove them from the pan with a slotted spoon.

In a mixing bowl, toss the cooked *pancetta* with the bread crumbs, *parmigiano*, garlic, parsley, salt, and pepper. Drizzle the broth over the mixture and toss to distribute evenly, then drizzle in the oil and toss again. Set the mixture aside.

To prepare the artichokes, cut off and discard the artichoke stems so the artichokes sit flat. On a cutting board, turn the artichokes on their side and cut off the top inch (2.5 cm) or so of each artichoke with a sharp knife. With scissors, snip 1/2" (12 mm) off all remaining leaf tips.

Sit the artichokes upright and gently open all leaves slightly with your thumbs. Pull out the pointed purple and yellow leaves from the centre of each artichoke to expose the fuzzy choke. Scoop out the all of the choke using a serrated grapefruit spoon or a melon-baller. Rinse the artichokes to remove any residue from the choke, then drizzle some lemon juice in the cavity of each artichoke.

Divide the stuffing into 4 equal portions. Spoon about 2 Tbsp. (30 ml) of stuffing into the cavity of each artichoke. Then, spread the leaves open as much as possible without breaking them and spoon a little of the stuffing throughout the leaves. After all of the stuffing has been tucked in, sprinkle each artichoke with a quarter of the grated *fontina*.

To cook the stuffed artichokes, put the water, wine, oil, bay leaf, lemon slices, garlic, peppercorns and salt in a saucepan or Dutch oven large enough to hold the artichokes in one layer. Carefully set the stuffed artichokes upright in the liquid, stem side down.

Bring the liquid just to a boil, then reduce the heat to simmer, cover the pot and simmer the artichokes for 50–55 minutes (depending on the size of artichokes). Check periodically and add a little more water if it looks like it might dry out before the end of the cooking time.

The artichokes are cooked when the leaves can be easily pulled out with a gentle tug and the edible lower portion of the artichoke is tender. Lift them out of the pot with a slotted spoon and place them in individual soup bowls. Strain any remaining cooking broth through a sieve and spoon the strained broth around the artichokes. Serve immediately.

Funghi al forno
ROASTED WILD MUSHROOMS

serves 4–6

*While not a mushroom lover, I remember fondly childhood excursions into nearby forests with "the adults"
to collect the thimble-sized wild mushrooms we called "stompini". The tidy chestnut-brown little caps perched on the stubby stems
grew in little colonies on the damp forest floor around tree stumps and were a much-anticipated seasonal treat
for all of the funghi fans in the family. A portion of each harvest would be prepared and enjoyed freshly cooked the day of picking;
the remainder would be preserved as a winter treat or for use in making antipasto.*

*The usual cautions about wild mushrooms apply; if you are not absolutely confident they are edible, or
if you do not have access to a local wild mushroom supply, porcini mushrooms are now generally available in most markets.*

4–5 cups (1 l–1.2 l) wild mushrooms,
    tops peeled, stems scraped and
    damaged parts removed and
    discarded
2 garlic cloves, minced
2 tsp. (10 ml) *pesto di verdure* **or**
    1 tsp. (5 ml) Italian seasoning
salt and freshly ground pepper
2 Tbsp. (30 ml) extra virgin olive oil
1 cup (250 ml) chicken or beef broth
1 cup (250 ml) white wine
fresh Italian parsley, coarsely chopped

Wash the mushrooms carefully and rinse twice or more until the water is clear of any residue.

Set the mushrooms in a large pot with about 1" (2.5 cm) of water, heat to medium and cook for 3-4 minutes. Drain the mushrooms and rinse them well again.

Preheat the oven to 300° F (150° C).

In a large pan or casserole dish, add the garlic, *pesto*, salt, pepper and oil and toss the mushrooms in this mixture to coat.

Cook the mushrooms in the warmed oven for 1/2 hour, stir well and add 1/2 cup each of broth and wine. Taste and adjust for salt and pepper.

Cook for a further 1 1/2 hours, adding the remaining broth and wine halfway through the cooking time and stirring periodically. Garnish with parsley and serve hot.

The ovens of Antrodoco

My husband and I made our first trip to Antrodoco in the mid 1970s during the Easter season and we will never forget seeing the procession of sturdy women, walking one behind the other in slow sure steps as they balanced a long wide plank on their heads. On the plank, set on colourful hand-stitched cloths, were twelve circular high-sided baking pans filled with perfectly-risen *pane di Pasqua* (Easter bread). The golden, rounded mounds had a satiny sheen and some were flecked with colourful candied fruits, others with plump raisins.

We managed to convince the women to slow down just long enough for us to snap a few pictures but they were on a purposeful mission and did not allow themselves to be distracted by the curiosity of two young travelers. Their destination was the large communal ovens which, just as they had been for centuries, were fired up and ready to transform the sweet dough into the aromatic and festive traditional bread of Easter.

We watched as each pan was gently slid into the large cavity of the brick oven and we lingered there to catch the wonderful, familiar aroma of anise, lemon and citron as the loaves baked. I imagined Nonna here, first as a child helping in the preparations, then, when she was tall enough, as one of the women in the annual Easter season procession. I thought about Nonna's kitchen in her new North American home and appreciated in a way I hadn't before why Nonna held on to her wood burning stove long after electric ranges had taken their place in most other kitchens.

The women of Antrodoco balance pane di Pasqua, *in the annual Easter season procession.*

Bread and pizza recipes

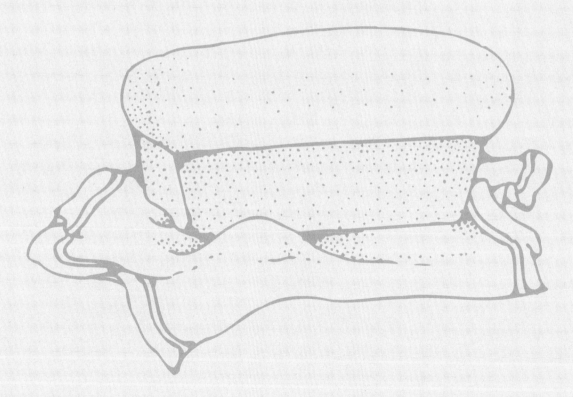

Pane di Pasqua
EASTER BREAD

makes 7–8 loaves

This is a light, slightly sweet bread with a soft ivory colour.
It is delicious served fresh, but if you toast it, you are rewarded with the irresistible and distinctive aroma of anise
which will permeate your kitchen. Easter bread also freezes well.

1 1/2 cups tepid water (110°–115° F; 60°–65° C)

3 tsp. (15 ml) sugar

3 packages dried yeast **or** 1/4 lb. (125 g) fresh yeast

2 cups (500 ml) sugar

1/2 lb. (250 g) butter

8 large eggs, room temperature

1 tsp. (5 ml) salt

1 tsp. (5 ml) anise extract

1 oz. (30 g) rum or brandy

1 tsp. (5 ml) *spumadoro* (if available)

2 cups (500 ml) milk, scalded then cooled to tepid

13 – 14 cups (2.6 l. to 3.5 l) flour

finely grated rind of 1 lemon and 1 orange

7 bread pans, greased

1 egg, lightly beaten **or** 1/2 cup (125 ml) milk

Put the tepid water into a warmed bowl and stir in the sugar. Sprinkle the yeast over the water and set the mixture aside in a warm, draft-free place for 10 minutes to activate the yeast. If the yeast does not froth up, discard it and start again with some fresh yeast.

In a medium mixing bowl, cream the butter and sugar well for 3 or 4 minutes. Add the eggs, one at a time, beating after each addition. Mix in the anise extract, rum or brandy, salt and *spumadoro* (if available).

When the yeast has risen, add the tepid milk to the egg-butter mixture, stirring, and then stir in the risen yeast. Keep this mixture warm and draft-free.

In a large bowl, sift 8 cups (2 l) of the flour and mix in the grated lemon and orange rind. Make a well in the centre of the flour and pour in the egg-yeast mixture. Mix well with a wooden spoon, incorporating all of the flour.

Sift in the remaining flour a little bit at a time, incorporating the flour after each addition with a wooden spoon and then your hands when it gets too hard to mix with a spoon. Add only enough additional flour until the dough is no longer sticky.

Place the dough on a floured board. Cover it with a tea towel and let it rest in a warm, draft-free place for 10 minutes. Grease

Continued on next page

your hands, remove the towel and knead the dough for at least 20 minutes until it is smooth. Cover and let it rise in a draft-free warm place for 2 hours.

Punch it down, cover it and let it rest for a few minutes, then separate the dough into 7 equal pieces. Shape the pieces into loaves and place them in greased pans.

Cover and let the loaves rise in a warm draft-free place for 2 hours or until doubled. Brush the tops with beaten egg or milk.

Preheat the oven to 325° F (160° C). Bake the risen loaves for 35–40 minutes. Remove the loaves from the oven and cool them on racks. When completely cooled, store in airtight bags.

Bread dough

makes 2 large loaves

Every Italian kitchen has a favourite bread recipe.
This is my mother's recipe for white bread which she uses for loaves as well as for making pizze fritte *(see p. 110).*

3/4 cup plus 3 Tbsp. (225 ml) tepid
    water (105°–115° F/40°–50° C)
1 tsp. (5 ml) sugar
1 pkg. active dried yeast **or** 1 oz. (30 g)
    fresh yeast
3 cups (750 ml) unbleached flour
1 tsp. (5 ml) salt
oil for greasing

Combine the tepid water and sugar in a warmed bowl and sprinkle the yeast over it. Whisk it until the yeast is dissolved. Cover it and let the mixture stand in a warm place for 10-15 minutes until it is frothy on the surface. (If it doesn't get frothy, start again with some different yeast.)

Sift 2 cups (500 ml) of the flour and salt into a large bowl. Make a well in the centre and pour in the yeast mixture. Using floured hands or a wooden spoon, mix it together to form a sticky dough.

Turn the dough out onto a floured board and gradually work in only as much of the remaining flour as is necessary to eliminate stickiness. Knead it for 10 minutes or until it is smooth and elastic.

Put the dough into a lightly greased warmed bowl, turn the dough over so that all sides are lightly oiled, cover the bowl and let the dough rise in a warm, draft-free place for 2 hours or until doubled in size.

Turn the dough out onto a lightly floured board and punch it down. Knead it 4 or 5 times, then separate it into two pieces and shape it into bread loaves (or use unbaked dough for *Pizze Fritte*.)

Place the loaves into greased baking tins, cover and let them rise in a warm, draft-free place until doubled. Bake the loaves in a preheated 325° F (160° C) oven for 30–35 minutes and cool on racks before slicing or storing.

Pizze fritte
BREAD FRITTERS

makes 10–12

Whenever Nonna made bread, she usually reserved some dough to make these decadent-but-worth-it little treats.
My mother continued the tradition, much to our delight as we arrived home for lunch on bread-making day!

1 loaf unbaked bread dough

3" (7.5 cm) of vegetable oil in a deep heavy pot or a deep-fryer

1/2 cup (125 ml) sugar and 1 tsp. (5 ml) cinnamon, mixed together

Cut off pieces of bread dough about the size of an egg. Shape each piece into an oval of consistent 1/4" (6 mm) thickness.

Heat the oil to medium-high. Fry the *pizze*, one at a time, in the oil, turning once, and remove them from the oil as soon as the bread is golden and puffy.

Place the *pizze fritte* on a bed of paper towels or a clean cloth and turn them a few times to soak up any excess oil. Put the cinnamon-sugar on a flat plate and gently press each side of the *pizze fritte* in the sugar, shaking off any excess. Serve immediately.

On our first trip to Antrodoco in 1977, we encountered this procession of women carrying the loaves of risen pane di Pasqua *(Easter bread)* to the communal oven.

Small colourful morsels of raisins and candied fruits are often added to this lightly sweet, anise-flavoured bread.

(See Pane di Pasqua *page* 107.)

A lush grove of castagne *trees forms the backdrop for this typical scene from the town of Antrodoco.*

Castagne *are collected in the early fall and dried, in preparation for use in making paste for baking or for roasting after a winter meal.*

(*See* Castagne, *page 118.*)

Pizza dough

makes one 10" x 14" (25 cm x 36 cm) thick-crust pizza shell
or one 11" x 17" (28 cm x 43 cm) thin-crust shell

This is an easy and versatile dough which can be used with a variety of toppings.

3/4 cup (180 ml) warm
    water
1 1/2 tsp. (7 ml) active
    dry yeast
1 tsp. sugar
2 cups (500 ml)
    unbleached
    all-purpose flour
1 tsp. (5 ml) salt
extra virgin olive oil

In a warmed bowl, stir together the water and the yeast until the yeast is dissolved. Sprinkle in the sugar and stir again. Let the mixture sit, covered, in a warm draft-free place for 8 to 10 minutes or until the yeast becomes frothy. If the yeast does not become frothy, discard it and try again with fresh yeast.

In a large bowl whisk together the flour and the salt. Make a well in the centre and pour the yeast mixture into the well, stirring with a wooden spoon or your hands just until a soft, messy and still a bit sticky dough forms. On a lightly floured surface knead the dough for about 10 minutes with lightly greased hands until it is smooth and elastic.

Transfer the dough to a large, warmed, lightly oiled bowl and turn the dough over so that all sides are lightly oiled. Cover the bowl with plastic wrap and a towel and let the dough rise in a warm draft-free place for about 1 1/2 hours or until it doubles in size.

Generously grease a 10" x 14" (25 cm x 36 cm) pan, for a thick-crust pizza or an 11" x 17" (28 cm x 43 cm) pan for a thin crust pizza.

On a lightly floured surface flatten the dough with your hands and stretch it into a rectangle. Lift the rectangle onto the greased pan and stretch it to the inside edges of the pan. Grease your hands and run them all over the top of the dough to grease it lightly.

Cover the pan loosely with plastic wrap, leaving room for the dough to expand, then with a light towel, and let it rise again in a warm draft-free place for one hour or until it doubles in size. Top it with your favourite toppings and let it rise again for 15 minutes, then bake it in a preheated oven at 350° F (180° C) for 35–45 minutes (for thick crust) or 15–20 minutes (for thin crust).

Thick-crust pizza with anchovies, peppers and tomatoes

makes one 10" x 14" (25 cm x 36 cm) thick crust pizza

Nonna's pizza bore little resemblance to the pizza parlour version with thick layers of toppings and cheese.
She used good quality toppings sparingly so that they complemented the soft chewy bread.

The vegetables for this thick crust pizza should be sliced very thinly so that they become slightly chewy in the cooking process.

one pizza dough recipe, risen once, stretched into a 10" x 14" (25 cm x 36 cm) well-greased pan and risen a second time

3 Tbsp. (45 ml) extra virgin olive oil

2 Tbsp. (30 ml) tomato paste mixed with 2 Tbsp. (30 ml) water

2 tsp. (10 ml) dried oregano

1 tsp. crushed hot chilli peppers (optional)

5 or 6 anchovy fillets, drained and separated

1 ripe plum tomato, thinly sliced into rounds

1/2 of a medium green pepper, thinly sliced crosswise into rounds

salt and pepper

1/2 cup (125 ml) shredded *pecorino*, *romano* or *parmigiano* cheese

Preheat the oven to 350° F (180° C).

Brush the top of the risen dough gently with the tomato paste mixture, then drizzle the olive oil over it and brush again lightly to distribute the oil. Sprinkle the oregano and chilli flakes (if using) over the oil.

Arrange the thin tomato slices over the dough (don't overlap them), followed by the anchovy filets, then the green pepper slices. Do not overlap the ingredients. Dust it with salt and a light grinding of black pepper.

Sprinkle the shredded cheese over everything. Cover the pizza with a clean cloth and let it sit for 15–20 minutes in a warm, draft-free place.

Remove the cloth and bake the pizza for 35–40 minutes at 350° F (180° C) or until the cheese has turned golden and the surface is lightly crusty but not dry. Slice into squares to serve.

Thin-crust pizza with pancetta and roasted garlic

makes one 11" x 17" (28 cm x 43 cm) pizza

My husband, Bruce, created this intensely-flavoured topping for a thin crust pizza. Pancetta is available in many delis and most Italian markets.

three 1/2" (1.2 cm) thick slices of *pancetta*, diced

one head of garlic, roasted (p. 32)

one pizza dough recipe, risen once, stretched into an 11" x17" (28 x 43 cm) well-greased pan and risen a second time

5 Tbsp. (75 ml) tomato paste mixed with 5 Tbsp. (75 ml) water

3 Tbsp. (45 ml) extra virgin olive oil

2 tsp. (10 ml) dried oregano

1 tsp. crushed hot chilli peppers

1 ripe plum tomato, thinly sliced into rounds

salt and freshly ground pepper

3/4 cup (180 ml) shredded *pecorino*, *romano* or *parmigiano* cheese

Preheat the oven to 350° F (180° C).

In a medium sauté pan, sauté the diced *pancetta* over medium heat until well-browned. Remove with a slotted spoon to a piece of absorbent paper and set aside.

Remove the cloves from the roasted garlic, peel them carefully and set them aside.

Brush the top of the risen dough gently with the tomato paste mixture, then drizzle the olive oil over it and brush again lightly to distribute the oil. Sprinkle the oregano and chilli flakes over the oil.

Arrange the thin tomato slices over the dough (don't overlap them), then distribute the diced *pancetta* and the roasted garlic cloves. Dust the pizza with salt and several generous grindings of black pepper.

Sprinkle the shredded cheese over everything. Cover the pizza with a clean cloth and let it sit for 15–20 minutes in a warm, draft-free place.

Remove the cloth and bake the pizza for 15 minutes at 350° F (180° C) or until the cheese has turned golden and the surface is lightly crusty. Slice into squares to serve.

Bruschetta

TOMATO BASIL TOASTS

makes 18–20 slices

*When the tomatoes are at their plumpest red, there are few better ways to enjoy them
than mounded on top of little garlicky toasted bread slices.
Choose a dense, chewy bread—an airy bread doesn't provide the right consistency and can get soggy.*

1 long baguette-type Italian bread, sliced into 1/2" (1.2 cm) slices

2 Tbsp. (30 ml) extra virgin olive oil

3 large garlic cloves, crushed with the side of a wide knife (but not chopped)

3 ripe red tomatoes, seeded, drained and diced into 1/4" (6 mm) cubes

10–12 leaves fresh basil, chopped finely

salt and freshly ground pepper

2 Tbsp. (30 ml) grated *fontina* or *asiago* cheese (optional)

Preheat the oven to 350° F (180° C).

Place the bread slices on a cookie sheet and toast them in the oven on both sides to a light golden colour. Remove them from the oven and rub each bread slice with a crushed garlic clove. Discard the garlic. Brush each slice with olive oil and set aside.

Toss the basil and diced tomatoes together. Salt and pepper to taste. Mound a tablespoon (15 ml) of tomato-basil mixture on each bread slice.

Serve the *bruschetta* immediately or, if using cheese, sprinkle some grated cheese over the tomato-basil mixture and place the *bruschetta* under a hot oven broiler for a minute or so, just until the cheese is melted. Serve immediately.

Copetta chronicles

FOR EVERYDAY MEALS, dessert at Nonna's house was usually simple. When the peaches were at their juiciest freshness, they were sliced at the table into a glass of red wine. After soaking for a few minutes they were speared with a fork and eaten with gusto—by adults and children alike. During the winter months when fresh fruit was scarce, we munched on dried figs or tucked into a batch of roasted chestnuts. Nonna always had a supply of fresh baking stored in her pantry to arrange the plate of "*i dolcei*" to enjoy with the after dinner coffee—*biscotti* for dunking, sticky *scallili* for a finger-licking treat, *ferratelle* for nibbling. Special occasions called for specialty dishes, such as *piatto forte*.

One of the most sought-after sweets was *copetta*—a chewy honey and nut confection which was cut into diamonds and stored on waxed paper with bay leaves in between. Making *copetta* required commitment. The honey had to be stirred constantly for a long time in order to achieve just the right consistency and colour. Although I eagerly awaited the appearance of the little amber-coloured diamonds on the dessert platter each year, I never had the patience—or foresight—to stand beside Nonna to learn her secret for making *copetta*. When Nonna died, my *copetta*-eating days ended.

I have been on a quest since then to learn to make it—a quest which is littered with many experimental pots of failed, sticky goo and the acrid smell of burnt nuts and honey in our kitchen; a quest which has driven me to search the internet and pore through cookbook indexes at bookstores, looking in vain under the letter "c." And I have not been alone in this journey. Cousin Don Poscente, a successful chocolatier and candy-maker in Toronto, has also been trying to crack the *copetta* code in his shop kitchen. Thanks to the guidance first of Aunty Mary and then of Giovanna Pascasi, our cousin who lives in Antrodoco and stills follows the tradition of making *copetta* for Christmas each year, there is a happy ending to this story. Nonna's *copetta* lives on.

In Antrodoco, Giovanna Pascasi and Val discuss rolling out the copetta.

Sweets and baked goods recipes

Copetta

HONEY AND NUT CONFECTION

makes approximately 40 diamonds

4 cups (1 l) liquid honey

1/2 cup (125 ml) sugar

2 1/2 cups (625 ml) finely chopped hazelnuts, almonds or walnuts

24–30 bay leaves

waxed paper

Wash the surface of a large wooden board (16" x 20"/ 40 cm x 50 cm or larger) with water and do not dry it. Have it ready on the counter or table, along with a moistened wooden rolling pin or a moistened wooden paddle.

In a heavy pot, ideally copper or copper-bottomed, heat the honey and sugar over a medium heat. Bring it just to, but not past, the point where there is the occasional bubble. Stir constantly for 30 minutes, adjusting the heat as necessary to maintain it at this occasional bubble. Carefully wipe away any sugar crystals which may form up the sides of the pan in the early stages of cooking so that they do not fall into the pot (they can cause the rest of the mixture to crystallize).

After 30–40 minutes, the mixture should be a rich golden colour. Add the nuts and reduce the heat slightly. Continue cooking and stirring the mixture for another 40–50 minutes, keeping it just below the boiling point (200° F/ 100° C). At the end of this cooking period, the *copetta* mixture will be the colour of mahogany and thickening, requiring a little more effort to stir. Remove the pot from the heat and let it cool and thicken in the pot for 10 minutes.

Remoisten the board if it has dried, then scrape the *copetta* onto the centre of the moistened board. Remoisten the rolling pin or paddle if it has dried (the water keeps it from sticking) and roll or press the *copetta* to a large mat approximately 1/4" (6 mm) thick.

Allow the *copetta* to cool for 10 minutes, then, using a sharp knife, carefully cut it into diamond shapes about 3" long and 2" wide (7.5 cm x 5 cm). Allow the *copetta* to cool completely before storing.

To store, arrange the *copetta* diamonds on waxed paper and place a bay leaf on top of each one. Cover with another layer of waxed paper.

To serve, peel the *copetta* off the waxed paper and peel off and discard the bay leaf.

Castagne
ROASTED CHESTNUTS

Overlooking Nonna's village of Antrodoco is a hill covered in a grove of edible chestnut trees.
After the harvest, the shiny brown seeds are laid out on the sidewalk and raked periodically so that they dry evenly.
Castagne are roasted and eaten after a winter meal, used in stuffings or made into a paste used in certain baked delicacies.

8–10 fresh chestnuts per person
(look for plump, firm ones of
uniform size with glossy shells)
1 cup (250 ml) red wine

Preheat the oven to 350° F (180° C).

With a sharp pointed knife, cut an "x" into the skin of each chestnut (this keeps it from exploding as it expands during cooking.) Place the chestnuts in a single layer in a roasting pan and roast them in a hot oven.

After 20 minutes, test one by removing it from the oven, rolling it on a board or table in a dampened cloth and peeling it. The flesh of the inner "nut" should be cooked through and have a consistency similar to that of a soft nut (pecan, cashew, walnut). Roast the remaining *castagne* for a further few minutes if required and test again.

When done, remove the *castagne* from the oven and wrap them in a clean but old towel. Sprinkle the towel with wine and press the towel-wrapped *castagne* against a board or table, rolling and pressing to crack the shells and make them easier to peel.

Put the *castagne* into a bowl and serve (have a spare empty bowl ready for the shells as people peel them).

Cousin Eugenio gathers chestnuts into a roasting pan to prepare them for dessert after lunch in Antrodoco.

Pane di spagna
SPONGE CAKE)

makes one 10" (25 cm) cake

*Sponge cake is a versatile sweet which is delicious on its own
or for use in layered desserts such as* tiramisu *or one of Nonna's specialties,* piatto forte.

1 1/3 cups (330 ml) flour

1 1/4 cups (310 ml) sugar

8 large eggs, at room temperature, separated into yolks and whites

2 Tbsp. (30 ml) water

2 tsp. (10 ml) grated lemon rind

1 tsp. (5 ml) vanilla extract or almond extract

1 Tbsp. (15 ml) icing sugar (optional)

Pre-heat the oven to 325° F (160° C).

In a mixing bowl, sift 1/2 cup (125 ml) of sugar with flour, then sift a second time to ensure the sugar and flour are well blended.

In a separate large bowl, beat together the yolks, water, lemon rind and vanilla extract until well blended (3–4 minutes). Gradually sift the flour-sugar mixture over the egg mixture, folding in gently while sifting. Set this mixture aside.

In a separate mixing bowl, beat the egg whites until foamy (3–4 minutes) and gradually add the remaining 3/4 cup (185 ml) of sugar, beating constantly until the egg whites form stiff peaks.

Gently fold the stiff egg whites into the flour-egg mixture just until incorporated. Pour the batter into an ungreased 10" (25 cm) cake pan or angel food cake pan.

Bake at 325° F (160° C) for 45 minutes or until the cake separates from the sides of the pan. When the cake is done, remove it from the oven and invert it on a wire rack to cool.

When cool, decorate the top of the cake with some sifted icing sugar if desired. Serve it with *gelato* and fresh berries or whipping cream and fresh peach slices or use it in recipes such as *piatto forte* or *tiramisu*.

Piattoforte

LAYERED DESSERT

serves 8–10

This "strong dish" was reserved for special occasions!
Savoiardi biscuits are available in any Italian market or deli.

For the chocolate custard:
4 Tbsp. (60 ml) sugar
1/3 cup (80 ml) unsweetened cocoa powder
3 Tbsp. (45 ml) cornstarch
2 cups (500 ml) whole milk or light cream
a pinch of cinnamon

For the vanilla custard:
2 Tbsp. (30 ml) sugar
3 Tbsp. (45 ml) cornstarch
2 cups (500 ml) whole milk or light cream
1 tsp. (5 ml) vanilla extract

For the layers:
3/4 cup (180 ml) red vermouth
3/4 cup (180 ml) light rum
1 package of *Savoiardi* biscuits **or** one day-old
  10" (25 cm) sponge cake, sliced horizontally
  into 2 layers
1 cup (250 ml) whipping cream
1/2 cup (125 ml) sliced almonds, lightly toasted
1 tsp. (5 ml) cinnamon

To make the chocolate custard:
Whisk together the sugar, cocoa and cornstarch in a medium saucepan. Gradually whisk in one cup of the cream or milk to form a smooth mixture, then whisk in the remaining cream or milk.

Set the pan on medium heat and cook, whisking constantly, until the mixture thickens and comes to a boil (about 5 minutes). Continue to whisk for a minute, then remove the pan from the heat. Stir in a pinch of cinnamon then cover the custard with plastic wrap, laying the wrap right on the surface of the custard (to prevent a skin from forming as it cools). Set aside to cool.

To make the vanilla custard:
Whisk together the sugar and cornstarch in a medium saucepan. Proceed to mix in the cream or milk and cook as with the chocolate custard. Stir in the vanilla after removing the custard from the heat, then cover and cool as with the chocolate custard. Set aside.

Piatto forte

Continued

To assemble the piatto forte:

Put one layer of *savoiardi* biscuits into the bottom of a 10" (25 cm) pan (or create a layer with one slice of cake). Sprinkle 1/2 of the vermouth and 1/2 of the rum over the layer.

Spoon the cooled vanilla custard over the biscuits or cake and carefully spread to cover. Create a second layer of *savoiardi* biscuits (or cake) over the custard, sprinkle the remaining rum and vermouth over it and spoon and spread the chocolate custard to cover.

Refrigerate the *piatto forte* for a few hours. Just before serving, whip the cream until thick and spoon and spread it gently over the chocolate layer. Decorate the top with sliced almonds and a sprinkle of cinnamon (optional). Cut the *piatto forte* into squares and use a lifter to serve.

Tiramisu

ESPRESSO AND MASCARPONE DESSERT

serves 8–10

Another layered dessert which is built with sponge cake or savoiardi *biscuits,*
tiramisu *uses the creamy Italian* mascarpone *cheese. This favourite special-occasion recipe for* tiramisu *is a lighter version,*
using light cream cheese to replace half of the mascarpone. *It's also alcohol free.*

8 oz. (250 ml) *mascarpone* cheese

8 oz. (250 ml) low-fat cream cheese

3 eggs, separated into yolks and
   whites

1/2 cup (125 ml) sugar

1 package of *savoiardi* biscuits or a
   day-old 10" (25 cm) sponge cake,
   sliced horizontally into 2 layers

1 1/2–2 cups (375–500 ml) brewed
   espresso or other dark coffee,
   cooled

1 cup (250 ml) crushed *amaretti*
   cookie crumbs (12–15 *amaretti*)*

4 Tbsp. (60 ml) cocoa powder, sifted

Whisk the *mascarpone* and cream cheeses to a smooth consistency and set aside.

In a large bowl, beat the egg yolks and sugar for 7 or 8 minutes until smooth and pale yellow. Fold in the *mascarpone*/cheese mixture.

In a separate bowl, beat the egg whites until stiff. Gently stir 1/3 of the beaten egg whites into the egg-cheese mixture, then fold in the remaining whites.

If you are using *savoiardi* biscuits, put 1 cup (250 ml) of the coffee in a wide, shallow bowl, immerse each biscuit briefly in the coffee and remove it quickly so it doesn't get mushy. Arrange the dipped biscuits in the bottom of a 10" (25 cm) pan. (If using cake, put the cake slice in the bottom of the pan and sprinkle just enough coffee over the cake to make it moist but not mushy).

Spoon 1/2 of *mascarpone* **mixture** over this layer and carefully spread to cover. Sprinkle with 1/2 of the *amaretti* crumbs and dust with 2 Tbsp.(30 ml) of cocoa powder. (Put the cocoa in a tiny strainer and tap it to distribute the cocoa powder.)

Cover this layer with the second layer of savoiardi biscuits or cake and repeat the process (coffee/*mascarpone*/*amaretti*/chocolate). Refrigerate the *tiramisu* for several hours and keep it refrigerated until ready to serve.

> * *Note*: For a tidy and quick way to crush *amaretti*, put them in a ziploc bag and run the rolling pin over the bag a few times.

Ferratelle

SNOWFLAKE COOKIES

makes 10–12 dozen cookies, depending on size

*Nonna baked these cookies on the top of her wood stove using a molding iron forged by Mr. D'Archangelo,
who learned his craft in a little town in Abruzzo called Quadri Chieti. More commonly known as* pizzelle,
we knew these snowflake-shaped cookies as "ferratelle", likely a dialectical term derived from the word "ferro" or iron.

Pizzelle irons (electric or manual) can be found in most good Italian food stores.

6 eggs

1/2 cup (125 ml)
safflower or
vegetable oil

2 tsp. (10 ml) star
anise extract

3 cups (750 ml) flour

2 tsp. (10 ml) baking
powder

1 1/2 cups (375 ml)
sugar

*Uncle Dante
makes ferratelle*

Heat up the *pizzelle* iron according to operating instructions.

In a large mixing bowl, beat the eggs until smooth, add the oil and anise extract and beat to incorporate.

Whisk together the flour and baking powder, then gradually sift the flour mixture over the egg mixture, beating well after each addition until smooth. Add the sugar and mix until smooth. The consistency of the batter should be such that it drops in a slow ribbon from a spoon, leaving some batter behind on the spoon. If the batter is too thick, add a little bit of water and mix it again until the right consistency is achieved.

Drop the batter by teaspoonful (5 ml) onto a greased hot *pizzelle* iron and let it bake until the steam stops (about 20–30 seconds). The cookie should be a creamy colour. Carefully peel the cookie from the iron and place it on a rack to cool. You will need to experiment with the first few cookies to get the size and timing right. When completely cooled, store the cookies in an airtight container.

Note: To make chocolate *ferratelle*, melt 6 semi-sweet chocolate squares, drizzle the melted chocolate into the prepared batter and mix to incorporate evenly. Cook as for *ferratelle*.

Almond biscotti

TWICE-BAKED COOKIES

makes about 70 cookies

Now a common feature in North American coffee bars, biscotti have been a tradition for hundreds of years in Italy.
They store well and make great "dunkers" for coffee, tea or hot chocolate.
Nonna always had a supply of the tiny toasted mouthfuls in her pantry for unexpected guests.

The size of the cookies and the flavourings used are really a matter of taste. Following are two popular varieties.

3/4 cup (180 ml) butter

1 1/2 cups (375 ml) sugar

6 eggs

1 tsp. (5 ml) vanilla

2 tsp. (10 ml) star anise extract

4–5 cups (1–1.3 l) flour

3 tsp. (15 ml) baking powder

1/2 cup (125 ml) sliced almonds, lightly toasted

2 oz. (60 g) semi-sweet chocolate cubes, melted in the top of a double boiler (optional)

Preheat the oven to 350° F (180° C).

In a large bowl, cream the butter and sugar well. Stir in the vanilla and star anise. Add the eggs one at a time, beating well after each addition.

Gradually sift in the flour and baking powder, mixing with a wooden spoon when the batter is too stiff to mix with an electric mixer. Add just enough flour to make a soft dough which can be shaped into logs. Work in the sliced almonds.

Divide the dough into 4 equal pieces and shape each piece into a long, slightly flattened log about 12" (30 cm) long and 2" (5 cm) wide. Transfer the logs to a lightly greased baking sheet, leaving room between them as they will expand while baking.

Bake the logs in a preheated oven for 20–25 minutes or just until lightly golden. Remove the pan from the oven and let the logs cool for 5 minutes.

With a sharp knife (one with a serrated edge works well), cut each log into 1/2" (12 mm) slices on a slight angle to make small crescent-shaped cookies about 2–3" (5–7.5 cm) long.

Almond Biscotti

Continued

Arrange the slices on their sides on a greased cookie sheet and return them to the oven to bake 10 minutes on each side or until lightly toasted.

Cool the *biscotti* on a wire rack. If desired, decorate them with drizzled melted chocolate. (Dip a fork in the melted chocolate and shake the fork back and forth over the cookies to do this.)

Lemon poppyseed biscotti

makes about 70 cookies

Same ingredients as for almond *biscotti*, except:

grated zest from a large lemon

2 Tbsp. (30 ml) of poppyseeds instead of the sliced almonds

white chocolate instead of dark chocolate.

Follow the same method as for almond *biscotti* except:

❖ add grated zest from a large lemon with the eggs, and

❖ add 2 Tbsp. (30 ml) of poppyseeds with the dry ingredients *instead of* the sliced almonds, and

❖ decorate with melted white chocolate *instead of* dark chocolate.

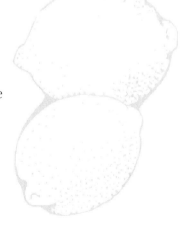

CRISPY BOWTIES

makes about 50 cookies

These light puffy delicacies are a special treat at Christmas time.

3 eggs

1/4 cup plus 2 tsp. (70 ml) sugar

1/4 cup (60 ml) white wine

1 Tbsp. (15 ml) each light rum and rye whiskey

1/2 cup (125 ml) butter, melted and cooled

juice and grated rind of 1 orange and 1/2 lemon

1 tsp. (5 ml) baking powder

1/2 tsp. (2 ml) salt

2–3 cups (.5–.75 l) flour

safflower or vegetable oil for deep-frying

berry sugar for dusting

With an electric mixer, beat the eggs well for about 10 minutes, add the sugar and continue beating for 5 minutes, then add the wine, rum and whiskey, melted butter and juice and grated rind while continuing to beat.

Combine the baking powder and salt with 1 1/2 cups (325 ml) of the flour and gradually beat this mixture into the egg mixture. Add another 1/2 cup (125 ml) of flour and continue mixing, using a wooden spoon when the dough becomes too hard to mix with a mixer.

Continue working in just enough flour just until the dough loses its stickiness and forms a soft ball which can be kneaded.

Knead the dough on a lightly floured surface for about 10 minutes or until it is smooth and pliable and bubbles start to form in the dough.

Put the dough in a lightly greased bowl, cover and let it rest for an hour.

Divide the dough into 5 or 6 rough balls. Working with 1 piece at a time and leaving the remaining balls in the covered bowl, roll it out on a lightly floured surface into a thin sheet about 1/16" (1.5 mm) thick or use a hand turned pasta machine to roll out the dough to the #6 thickness.

Lay the strip out on a towel-covered surface and let it rest, covered, while you roll out the remaining balls of dough.

Crostoli

Continued

When all of the dough has been rolled, take the first strip rolled and pass it through the #5 setting of the machine (or, if doing this by hand, pass the rolling pin over the strip with a gentle pressure).

Using a fluted pastry wheel (or a sharp knife), cut each strip into 3" x 1" (7.5 cm x 2.5 cm) strips. Make a 1" (2.5 cm) vertical cut in the centre of the strip and gently twist the strip. Cover the strips with a towel and let them rest while you prepare the oil.

Heat oil in large heavy saucepan or deep-fryer to a depth of 3" (7.5 cm). Fry the *crostoli*, a few at a time, turning them once, until they are puffy and golden (about 1/2 minute).

Drain the *crostoli* on absorbent paper, allow them to cool, then sprinkle with berry sugar.

Store in a tightly covered container.

Crostata di mandorle

ALMOND TART

makes 15–18 squares

This traditional tart can be made with an almond filling or any variety of good quality jam.

For the pastry:

1 1/2 cups (375 ml) all-purpose flour

1 cup (250 ml) cake flour (not self-rising)

1/3 cup (80 ml) sugar

1/4 tsp. (1 ml) salt

grated rind from one small lemon

3/4 cup plus 2 Tbsp. (210 ml) cold
    butter, cut into 1" (2.5 cm) cubes

1 large egg

1 large egg yolk

1 tsp. (5 ml) vanilla

1 tsp. (5 ml) lemon juice

For the filling:

3 egg whites

1 cup (250 ml) sugar

3 tsp. (15 ml) almond extract

1 cup (250 ml) ground almonds

To make the pastry:

Preheat the oven to 350° F (180° C). Lightly grease an 11" (28 cm) tart pan (one with a removable bottom is ideal) or a 9" x 9" (23 cm) square pan.

In a large mixing bowl, whisk together the flours, sugar, salt and grated lemon rind. With a pastry blender, cut in the butter cubes until the mixture resembles coarse meal.

In a pourable cup, lightly beat the whole egg and the yolk with a fork and mix in the vanilla. Gradually pour the eggs into the flour mixture, stirring to distribute and incorporate.

Stir in the lemon juice and with lightly greased hands gently work the dough just until it forms a smooth loose ball.

Remove a generous handful of the dough, shape it into a ball and flatten it into a thin disk. Wrap it in plastic wrap and refrigerate it while working with the remaining dough.

With lightly floured hands, roll 1/4 of the remaining dough into one or two long ropes the thickness of a pencil. Press the remaining dough evenly over the bottom (not up the sides) of the prepared tart pan. Lay the rolled rope around the edge of the dough, and press gently against the sides of the pan to form thin side walls for the *crostata*.

Crostata di mandorle

Continued

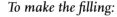

To make the filling:

Beat the egg whites until they form soft peaks, add the sugar and almond extract and beat to incorporate. Fold in the ground almonds.

Spread the filling over the dough. Roll out the reserved refrigerated dough to 1/4" (6 mm) thickness and cut it into 1/3" (8 mm) wide long strips. Starting with a short strip laid diagonally across one corner, gently arrange the strips over the filling in a lattice design.

To finish, lay a strip all around the inside edge of the crust (like a thin frame). Lightly beat the reserved egg yolk and 1 tsp. (5 ml) of cold water with a fork and brush it carefully over the lattice strips.

Bake the *crostata* for 40–45 minutes at 350° F (180° C) or until the lattice is shiny and golden. Cool and slice into thin wedges to serve.

Crostata d'albicocca

APRICOT TART

makes 15–18 squares

Same ingredients as for almond *biscotti*, except:

instead of the almond-egg white filling:

- 1 1/2 cups (375 ml) apricot preserves (homemade or a good-quality commercial variety with lower sugar content)
- 1/4 tsp. almond extract over the prepared pastry.

Follow the same method as for *Crostata di mandorle* but **instead** of the almond-egg white filling, mix 1 1/2 cups (375 ml) apricot preserves with 1/4 tsp. almond extract, and spread over the prepared pastry.

Finish with a lattice and bake in the same way.

Bignè alla panna
CREAM PUFFS

makes about 18 large cream puffs or 30 small

For the pastry:

1 cup (250 ml) hot water

1/4 lb. (125 g) butter

1 cup (250 ml) flour, sifted after measuring

4 large eggs, cracked into an easy-pour container (such as a liquid measuring cup)

Preheat the oven to 400° F (200° C). Lightly grease two cookie sheets.

In a medium size heavy pot bring the water and butter to a full boil. Add the flour all at once and stir with a wooden spoon until the mixture leaves the sides of the pot and forms a ball. Remove the pot from the heat at once and let it cool for 5 minutes.

Pour the eggs in one at a time, beating each one in thoroughly with a wooden spoon before adding the next.

When all the eggs have been incorporated, drop the batter by tablespoonful (15 ml) onto prepared cookie sheets, allowing room for spreading.

Bake in a preheated 400° F (200° C) oven for 10 minutes, reduce the oven temperature to 350° F (180° C) and bake for a further 30–35 minutes or until the puffs are crisp and light brown.

Remove them from the oven, turn the oven off and immediately make small slits in the side of each puff to allow the steam to escape. Return the puffs to the turned-off oven for 3 or 4 minutes to dry them a little more.

Using a sharp knife, neatly slice the top third of the top of each puff partly through so that the top forms a "lid" which can be folded back while filling.

When ready to serve, fill the puffs with whipped cream or your favourite custard or one of the following fillings. Finish with a dusting of powdered unsweetened cocoa mixed with powdered sugar or drizzle the tops with melted semi-sweet chocolate.

Chocolate custard filling

4 Tbsp. (60 ml) sugar

1/3 cup (80 ml) unsweetened cocoa
powder

3 Tbsp. (45 ml) cornstarch

2 cups (500 ml) whole milk or light
cream

a pinch of cinnamon

2 oz. (56 g) semi-sweet chocolate
squares, broken into several pieces

1/4 cup (60 ml) icing sugar and
1/4 cup (60 ml) unsweetened cocoa
powder, whisked together

Whisk together the sugar, cocoa and cornstarch in a medium saucepan.
Gradually whisk in one cup of the cream or milk to form a smooth mixture,
then whisk in the remaining cream or milk.

Set the pan on medium heat and cook, whisking constantly, until the mixture
thickens and comes to a boil (about 5 minutes). Continue to whisk for a
minute, then remove the pan from the heat. Stir in a pinch of cinnamon and
the pieces of chocolate squares until melted. Cover the custard with plastic
wrap, laying the wrap right on the surface of the custard (to prevent a skin
from forming as it cools). Set aside to cool.

Fill the puffs when ready to serve and finish the tops with a dusting of cocoa
powder and icing sugar or drizzle melted chocolate over them.

Chocolate-*ricotta* filling

1 lb. (500 g) *ricotta*

1 large orange with a healthy bright
orange skin

6 sugar cubes

2 oz. (60 g) semi-sweet chocolate,
chopped or grated into rice-sized
pieces

1 Tbsp. (15 ml) *Amaretto* (Italian liqueur)
or 1 tsp. (5 ml) almond extract

3 Tbsp. (45 ml) cream, approximately

1/4 cup (60 ml) icing sugar and
1/4 cup (60 ml) unsweetened cocoa
powder, sifted or whisked together

Put the *ricotta* in a fine strainer and let it sit over a bowl for 1/2 hour to drain.
Discard any liquid.

Wash the orange well and dry. Rub the sugar cubes firmly all over the orange,
soaking the orange oils into the sugar. (The rest of the orange is not used in
this recipe but can be saved and squeezed for orange juice.) Crush the sugar
cubes using a mortar or the back of a heavy spoon and reserve.

In a mixing bowl, combine the drained ricotta, the crushed sugar cubes, the
Amaretto and 2 Tbsp. (30 ml) of the cream and whisk until well combined.
The mixture will be smooth with small lumps. Taste and add more sugar if
necessary. Add the chocolate pieces and the remaining cream (if necessary to
make it creamier), and stir to combine. Refrigerate for 1/2 hour or more.

Fill the puffs when ready to serve and finish the tops with a dusting of cocoa
powder and icing sugar.

Amaretti

ALMOND MERINGUE COOKIES

makes about 48 cookies

These popular crunchy and chewy little cookies can be found in most Italian homes and vary in size, shape and texture, depending on the regional and family tradition. "Amaro" means bitter and these cookies are so-called because they are traditionally made with bitter almonds or bitter apricot pits. A few drops of bitter almond extract can produce a similar result.

Amaretti are delicious on their own or crumbled and used in baked apples, over ice cream or in a variety of pastries and desserts.

2 cups (500 ml) unblanched almonds
2 egg whites
1 cup (250 ml) berry sugar
2 Tbsp. (30 ml) flour
2 tsp. (10 ml) almond extract
1 tsp. (5 ml) baking powder

Preheat oven to 350 F (180 C). Grease two cookie sheets, dust them lightly with flour and shake off any residual flour.

In a food processor or by hand, finely chop the almonds and set aside.

In a large bowl, beat the egg whites until soft peaks form. Beat in the sugar, a little at a time, incorporating well after each addition before adding the next one. When all of the sugar has been incorporated, the mixture should be thick and shiny and ribbons should fall from the beaters when lifted.

Stir in the almonds, flour, almond extract and baking powder.

Drop the batter by level tablespoonfuls (15 ml) onto prepared cookie sheets, leaving room for spreading. Lightly press the cookies into tidy circles with your fingers.

Bake on the middle oven rack for about 20 minutes or until the cookies are lightly browned and crisp on top.

Let the *amaretti* cool on the pans for a few minutes, then lift them on to racks to cool completely.

Store in an airtight container.

In the cellar

PAPA AND NONNA'S CELLAR was a constantly-changing place. During the harvest season, the shelves in the cellar pantry gradually filled up with colourful jars of canned peaches, apricots, cherries, pickled beets, peppers, *antipasto*, *pestos*, tomatoes, *conserva*, mushrooms, and pickled trout. Then, over the winter months, Nonna dispatched us, by turns, to the cellar to collect the ingredients for this sauce or that dish — and the jars thus made

their way to the kitchen until the pantry shelves were, by the next harvest, ready to receive their new bounty. Next door to the pantry, Papa's wine cellar also followed an annual cycle — that of the grape-harvest and wine-making. Bottles of maturing wine and oak barrels lined the wine-cellar walls and a supply of empty bottles sat ready. Each fall, the old wooden grape-press, quiet and still the rest of the year, was reactivated and put to work crushing the grapes and starting this year's wine-making.

The cool darkness of the root cellar provided an eerie but ideal environment to store the root vegetables, such as carrots and potatoes. Nonna used only old potatoes to make her *gnocchi* as newer potatoes are too moist. On *gnocchi*-making days, the children would try to avoid being enlisted by Nonna to collect the potatoes, a gruesome experience of reaching into the dark barrel to locate the oldest, usually-rooting tubers. All that sustained the reluctant gatherer was the prospect of sitting down to a mouthwatering platter of fresh *gnocchi*!

Papa Vincenzo tests the wine

Pesto and preserves recipes

The young apprentice learns from his Nonno.

Nonna Sofia's son, Julio, guides his grandson, J.J., as they make jelly together.

The walls of Nonna and Papa's cellar were filled up with preserves, pickles and pestos in the summer months, ready for use over the winter in baking (as in crostata d'albicocca, page 129), appetizers (see Antipasto, page 138) or in soups and sauces (see In the cellar, page 133).

Buon appetito! *Nonna's great-granddaughter Niki displays a pan of* stracci, *an Abruzzese specialty and an enduring tradition in the kitchen of each new generation.*

(See Stracci, *page 48.)*

Pesto di verdure

MIXED GREENS PESTO

makes approximately 2 cups (500 ml)

The word "pesto" comes from the verb "pestare" which means to grind or crush.
Traditionally, pesto-making was done by hand, using a mortar and pestle or a hand-turned food mill.
It has become a much less labour-intensive endeavour since the advent of the food processor.

This pesto uses a combination of fresh herbs and provides a richer and more intense flavour than dried herb mixes
when added to sauces or soups or stews. It is crucial that the fresh herbs are dried off well before being processed together to
prevent mould from developing. If storing it in the fridge, top up the jar from time to time with a thin layer of olive oil to preserve it.

4 large garlic cloves, finely minced

2 cups (500 ml) fresh spinach leaves, washed, well-dried, and stems removed

2 cups (500 ml) fresh Italian parsley, washed, well-dried, and stems removed

1 cup (250 ml) arugula leaves, washed, well-dried, and stems removed

1 cup (250 ml) fresh oregano leaves, washed and well-dried

1/2 cup (125 ml) fresh thyme leaves, washed, stemmed and well-dried

1/2 cup (125 ml) minced fresh chives

1 small carrot, peeled and finely grated or finely minced

4 Tbsp. (60 ml) freshly grated *parmigiano* cheese

2 tsp. (10 ml) salt

1 Tbsp. and 1 tsp. (20 ml) freshly squeezed lemon juice

1/3 cup plus 1 Tbsp. (100 ml) extra virgin olive oil

In a large bowl, toss all of the ingredients, except the oil, together. Process (or hand chop) until the mixture is finely minced.

With the processor on, slowly pour oil through the food chute and process until it is well blended. (Or, if you are making it by hand, drizzle the oil into the minced mixture while mixing steadily.)

To store, spoon the *pesto* into jars and freeze or spoon into ice-cube trays, freeze and store the cubes in a freezer bag.

Pesto di basilico

BASIL PESTO

makes approximately 2 cups (500 ml)

This pesto is delicious in tomato dishes or simply tossed with your favourite pasta.
It can also be spread on polenta crostini or toasted Italian bread slices,
sprinkled with grated cheese and broiled.

4 Tbsp. (60 ml) pine nuts, lightly toasted

4 large garlic cloves

6 cups (1.5 l) fresh basil leaves, washed and trimmed and well-dried

4 Tbsp. (60 ml) freshly grated *parmigiano* cheese

2 tsp. (10 ml) salt

1 Tbsp. plus 1 tsp. (20 ml) freshly squeezed lemon juice

6 Tbsp. (90 ml) extra virgin olive oil

Finely mince the garlic cloves and pine nuts together in a food processor or by hand.

Add the basil, cheese and lemon juice and process or chop until it is finely minced.

With the processor on, slowly pour the oil through the food chute and process until well blended (or, if you are making it by hand, drizzle the oil into the minced mixture while mixing steadily).

Store as for *pesto di verdure*.

Conserva

SUN-DRIED TOMATO PASTE

When the tomato plants were hanging with red and fully ripe tomatoes, Nonna would collect a big basket of them
to make her conserva *which she used throughout the rest of the year to enhance her sauces and soups.*
She would lay out the cooked tomato reduction on a board in the sun porch to dry out and allow the flavour and consistency
to deepen into a rich, sweet paste before storing it in jars. While tomato paste can be substituted for conserva *in most recipes,*
it is really worth going to the trouble of making conserva *to experience the difference.*

a large bowl of fresh, deep red and
    perfectly ripe tomatoes

coarse salt

extra virgin olive oil

several small sterilized jars and lids
    for preserving

Carefully examine the tomatoes and remove any blemishes or imperfections. Cut out and discard the stem and any white parts, then cut the tomato into 4 pieces and put them into a heavy pot large enough to hold all of the tomatoes.

Add 1 tsp. (5 ml) of coarse salt for every 4 or 5 tomatoes. Simmer the tomatoes gently for several hours, stirring periodically, until the tomatoes transform into a soft red pulp. When all of the excess liquid has cooked away, force the tomatoes through a fine sieve to eliminate the skins and seeds.

Place the puree in a large, shallow glass or pottery bowl and allow it to sit overnight on the counter, lightly covered with a teatowel. The next day, spread the mixture over a large wooden board if you have one or leave it in the bowl. Place the board or bowl in a sunny spot indoors.

Once the surface dries and becomes firm, cover the puree with coarse salt (the salt will draw the moisture from the tomatoes to create a dense puree). Leave the *conserva* to continue drying for another few days until it has turned into a thick, dense paste.

Carefully scrape off the salt layer and put the *conserva* in a bowl. Stir it well with a wooden spoon. Freeze the *conserva* in small freezer containers.

Once thawed, keep a partially used container of *conserva* refrigerated and cover the surface with olive oil.

Antipasto
MIXED VEGETABLE PRESERVE
makes approximately 20 pint jars

3 lbs. (1.5 kg) cauliflower flowerets

2 lbs. (1 kg) green beans, cleaned and sliced into 1" (2.5 cm) pieces

2 lbs. (1 kg) small dilling cucumbers, cleaned and trimmed **or** two 500 ml jars baby dill pickles, drained

2 lbs. (1 kg) pickling pearl onions, peeled and trimmed **or** three 375 ml jars pickled pearl onions, drained

3/4 cup (180 ml) extra virgin olive oil

3 lbs. (1.5 kg) mushrooms (optional), thinly sliced. If not using mushrooms, increase cauliflower and green beans by 1 lb. (500 g) each.

four 11 oz. (345 ml) bottles good quality catsup

one 11 oz. (345 ml) bottle chilli sauce

2 lbs. (1 kg) green peppers, trimmed, seeded and diced into 1/2" (12 mm) squares

2 lbs. (1 kg) red peppers, trimmed, seeded and diced into 1/2" (12 mm) squares

3/4 cup (180 ml) white vinegar

five 16 oz. (500 ml) tins pitted ripe black olives, well-drained

five 16 oz. (500 ml) jars pimento-stuffed green olives, well-drained

five 8 oz. (250 g) tins chunk light tuna, well-drained and broken into bite-sized chunks

two 3 oz. (85 g) tins anchovies, (optional) well-drained and sliced into 1" (2.5 cm) pieces

20 pint jars and lids, well-sterilized and kept hot

Blanch the cauliflower flowerets for 3 minutes, then plunge them in cold water to stop the cooking process. Drain and cut them into bite-sized pieces.

Blanch the sliced green beans for 4 minutes, plunge them in cold water and drain.

Slice the dill cucumbers or baby dill pickles into 1/4" (6 mm) slices. Set these prepared vegetables aside.

In a pot large enough to hold all of the antipasto ingredients, bring the olive oil to medium heat. Fry the mushrooms (if using) for 2-3 minutes, add the catsup and chilli sauce and the green and red pepper pieces, bring it all to a simmer and cook for 10-12 minutes, stirring periodically with a wooden spoon.

Add the vinegar and simmer for a further 10 minutes.

Add all of the prepared vegetables and the black and green olives to the pot and stir to distribute, then add the tuna and anchovies (if using) and stir to distribute. Simmer all together for a further 10 minutes.

Fill the hot sterilized jars with the hot *antipasto* mixture just to the bottom of the neck, wipe the rim clean, carefully place the cap on the jar and twist on the lid until firm but not tight.

Place the jars upright in one or more roasting pans or casserole dishes, add enough water to the pans to create a 1" (2.5 cm) bath and place the pans in a 300° F (150° C) oven for 15 minutes.

Carefully remove the pans from the heat and let the jars of *antipasto* cool completely at room temperature. Test to make sure that caps have sealed before storing. They should each make a popping sound during cooling and the caps should appear slightly concave and not sound hollow when tapped. Twist the lids so they are tight.

Store the *antipasto* in a cool, dark place until ready to use. Opened jars of partially-used *antipasto* should be refrigerated.

Appendices

Herbs, Spices and Nuts

The herbs, spices and nuts Nonna used were ones she learned about as a child growing up in Antrodoco. Nonna and Papa cultivated as many of them as possible in their own giardino in Trail but, being a cooler climate than their native Antrodoco, some had to be bought. In Antrodoco, most herbs, nuts and spices used are grown locally or in other parts of Italy. However, some, such as nutmeg and cinnamon are also imported.

The following list includes the herbs, spices, seeds and nuts Nonna used most frequently, as well as a few added through our own adaptations and experimentation. Herbs can be used fresh or dried, or pestos of favourite combinations can be preserved with a good quality olive oil.

Aglio garlic: a bulbous plant (*Allium sativa*) of southern Europe whose bulb-head separates into cloves with a distinctive strong odour and flavour. Often sautéed with onion in olive oil and/or butter as the first step in making sauces and used to flavour meats, vegetables and stews.

Alloro bay: an aromatic Mediterranean shrub (*Laurus nobilis*) from the laurel family. The diamond-shaped leaves are used to flavoured meats and stews. Also used to store *copetta* (a honey and nut confection).

Aneto dill: an aromatic herb (*Anethum graveolens*) of Europe and southern Asia. Seeds are used mainly for pickling and feathery leaves are sometimes used in salads or as a garnish.

Anice anise: an aromatic Mediterranean herb (*Pimpinella anisum*) in the parsley family. The oval-shaped seeds of the anise plant, as well as the oil of the seeds, are used in baking. *Anisette* is a liqueur flavoured with anise seed oil.

Basilico basil: an Asian aromatic herb (*Ocimum basilicum*) of the mint family. Used dried, fresh or in *pesto* to flavour sauces, stews, meats, and vegetables. Particularly complementary to tomatoes.

Camomilla chamomile: an aromatic perennial herb (*Chamaemelum nobile*) with feathery foliage and white and yellow flowers. The dried flower heads are used to make tea (considered to have medicinal qualities when sweetened with honey and served with love!).

Cannella cinnamon: the dried inner bark of a tropical Asian tree (*Cinnamomum genus*), ground and used as a spice in desserts and some sauces.

Capperi capers: the pickled flower bulbs of a Mediterranean shrub (*Caparis spinosa*). Used to flavour poultry, rabbit and fish.

Castagne chestnuts: the edible seed fruit of the chestnut tree (*Castanea*). Chestnuts are roasted or boiled and eaten whole, chopped and used in stuffings or preserved in honey. Paste made from the cooked and mashed chestnuts is also used in baking. *Continued on next page*

Chiodi di garofini cloves: the pungent, aromatic dried flower buds of an evergreen tree (*Syzgium aromaticum*) native to the Moluccas (the "Spice Islands"). Used to flavour stews and game.

Cipolla onion: a pungent edible bulb (*Allium cepa*) cultivated worldwide. Used extensively, particularly sautéed in olive oil or butter as the first step in making a sauce, soup or stew.

Finocchio fennel: an aromatic Eurasian plant (*Foeniculum vulgare*). Stalks and seeds are used in some soups and vegetable dishes.

Maggiorana marjoram: a fragrant and spicy herb of the *Origanum* family. Used in stews, stuffings, soups and sauces.

Mandorla almond: the nut from the deciduous almond tree (*Prunus dulcis*). Used chopped or ground in many desserts. Oil extract used as a flavouring and in liqueur.

Menta mint: an aromatic herb (*Mentha*). Used fresh or dried in teas as a digestive aid or in fish dishes.

Noce walnut: the nut from the deciduous walnut tree (*Juglans*). Used chopped or ground in desserts.

Noce moscata nutmeg: the hard, aromatic seed of the evergreen tree *Myristica fragrans*, native to the East Indies. Ground and used sparingly in desserts and cream sauces.

Nocciola hazelnut: the nut from the small hazel tree (*Corylus avellana*). Made into a paste, ground or chopped and used in baking. Oil extract used in flavouring and liqueur.

Origano oregano: a perennial Eurasian herb (*Origanum vulgare*) of the mint family with a distinctive taste and aroma. Used in flavouring sauces and meats.

Pepe forte dried and crushed hot chilli pepper and seeds: the hot-flavoured fruit of the pepper plant (*Capsicum frutescens*). Used according to taste in sauces.

Pignole pine nuts: the creamy, delicate edible seed of a variety of pine tree. Used in *pestos*, salads and desserts.

Prezzemolo parsley: a leafy green Eurasian herb (*Petroselinum crispum*). The Italian variety has broad, flat leaves and is used extensively in *pesto* or fresh in sauces, meat and fish dishes, soups, stuffings and as a garnish.

Rosmarina rosemary: a fragrant evergreen Mediterranean shrub (*Rosmarinus officinalis*) with an intense flavour. Used with rabbit, lamb, veal, pork, poultry and roasted vegetables.

Seme di papavero poppy seeds: the small black round seeds of the poppy flower (*Papaver*). Seeds or paste used in baking.

Salvia sage: an aromatic greyish-green herb (*Salvia*). Used to flavour stuffings, poultry.

Timo thyme: an aromatic Eurasian shrub (*Thymus*) with small, spicy leaves. Used in soups, sauces, meats, poultry, fish, game and vegetables.

Zafferano saffron: the dried aromatic and colour-concentrated stigmas of the *Crocus sativus* plant. Used as a mild flavouring and colour-enhancer in soups, fish dishes and *risotto*.

Pasta Shapes

Much of the pasta Nonna served was fatto a mano *(hand-made). The fine, silky sheets were cut into various shapes and in some cases filled with a savoury filling (as in* ravioli*). Nonna always made enough fresh pasta for the night's meal as well as some to dry and store in the pantry for a future meal. A portion of the fresh-cut pasta strips were also chopped into little* pastine *(small pasta) for soup. Store-bought varieties were usually those pasta shapes which were too finicky to make in quantity by hand.*

The pairing of pasta and sauce is important. Some shapes, such as orechietti*, are designed to cradle a little pool of the sauce while* spaghetti *or* linguine *rely on the sauce adhering uniformly to the flat or curved sides. Thin pasta such as* vermicelli *do best in a lighter broth-like sauce, while* linguine *and* fettucine *can handle thicker cream or meat sauces. Following is a list of the favourite shapes in Nonna's cucina.*

acini di pepe: "pepper berries," this pasta is so-named because its small, round or square shape resembles that of peppercorns. Used in soups.

agnolotti: small crescent-shaped "turnovers" filled with a meat or spinach and cheese stuffing.

bucatini: "small holes," these are round tubular noodles with a hole through the centre.

cappelletti: "little hats," these are small filled crescents whose two ends have been joined to form a circle shape. Often used in soups.

capelli d'angelo: "angel hair," a very thin noodle.

cicerciole: tiny squares of homemade *pastine*, an Abruzzese specialty.

ciufulitti: a cylindrical noodle, similar to bucatini, which is a specialty of Antrodoco.

farfalle: "butterflies," these are short wide noodles which are pinched together in the centre to resemble a bow or butterfly.

farfallette: small *farfalle*, used in soups.

fettucine: *fette* means slice, which is the way these flat ribbons of noodle are made by hand.

lasagne: wide, thin noodles, boiled and then baked in layers alternating with meat sauces and cheese.

linguini: noodles which are narrower than *fettucine* but wider than *spaghetti* or *tagliarine*.

maccheroni alla chitarra: thick noodles cut lengthwise by rolling over taut strings resembling those of a guitar. An Abruzzese specialty.

ravioli: square pasta packets filled with a meat or cheese stuffing.

rigatoni: wide, ribbed tubes about a half-finger in length.

spaghetti: round noodles, thicker than *spaghettini*.

spaghettini: thin round noodles, but thicker than *capelli d'angelo*.

stelle: "stars," these tiny star-shaped *pastine* are used in soups.

tagliarini: from the verb *tagliare* (to cut), these are hand- or machine-cut noodles the same thickness as *spaghetti* but with squared sides.

tagliatelle: hand- or machine-cut noodles the same thickness as *fettucine*.

tortellini: similar to *cappelletti* but larger and served with sauce.

tubettini: tiny pasta tubes cut in short lengths and used in soups.

vermicelli: similar to angel hair pasta.

Formaggio
CHEESE

Cheese is used extensively in Abruzzese cooking. The mountainous interior of Abruzzo is ideal for grazing the large herds of sheep and cattle whose milk is used to produce cheese for local use as well as for export to other regions of Italy and beyond. Following are a few types of cheese which are good to have on hand, ready to be sliced and eaten on their own, sprinkled over soups or pastas, or used in cooking.

Gorgonzola	a pungent, blue-veined, creamy-white pressed cheese. Eaten sliced, used sauces or crumbled over salads or *crostini*.
Mozzarella	a soft, mild, white cheese from cow's milk (called *scamorza* when made from buffalo milk). Good melting cheese on bread or in baked dishes.
Parmigiano-reggiano	a rich, slightly salty, hard cheese produced by hand by artisan cheesemakers according to traditional methods. Usually grated and sprinkled over pastas or soups or sliced thinly for an *antipasto* platter.
Pecorino	an almost-white firm cheese made from sheep's milk. When young, the *pecorino* is mild and melts well. Aged, the taste sharpens and is used as a grating cheese (see *romano*).
Provolone	a light yellow slicing cheese molded into balls. With age, taste sharpens and texture changes from soft to firm. Usually eaten sliced.
Ricotta	a fresh, moist unsalted cheese made from the whey drained off while making cheese such as *mozzarella*. Eaten sliced or used in sauces, baked dishes and desserts.
Romano	a sharp, salty hard grating cheese made from sheep's milk. Usually grated and used in soups and sauces.

Glossary of Italian Terms

Following are terms used frequently in this book.

a mano	by hand	*insalata*	salad	*pomodoro*	tomato
agnello	lamb	*inverno*	winter	*radicchio*	chicory; waxy, slightly bitter salad greens
al dente	cooked just until still slightly firm to the bite	*maiale*	pork		
		mangiare	to eat	*ragu*	sauce made with tomatoes and ground meat
al forno	oven-roasted	*minestra*	soup		
balsamella	white sauce made from butter, flour and milk or cream	*morbido*	soft	*ripieni*	stuffed or filled
		Natale	Christmas	*risotto*	Italian Arborio rice
		oglio	oil	*scallopine*	thin slices of meat, pounded flat
brodo	broth	*pancetta*	Italian bacon, salt-cured and air dried		
carne	meat			*soffritto*	sauteed mixture, usually of olive oil, onions and garlic
ceci	chick peas				
cena	dinner	*pane*	bread		
coniglio	rabbit	*panna*	cream	*spezzatini*	bite-sized pieces
cucina	kitchen or cooking	*Pasqua*	Easter	*sugo*	sauce; *ragu*
estate	summer	*pepe forte*	hot red pepper	*tacchino*	turkey
fagioli	dried beans	*pepe nero*	black pepper	*trota*	trout
fagiolini	fresh green beans	*peperoncini*	small pepper	*verdure*	greens or vegetables
gamberi	prawns	*peperone*	bell pepper	*vitello*	veal
giardino	garden	*picante*	hot, spicy	*zuppa*	soup
imbottiti	stuffed	*polenta*	coarsely ground cornmeal		
		pollo	chicken		

Tables

of Dry and Liquid Measurement Equivalents and Temperature Guide

Measurements for ingredients used in the recipes in this book are stated in both US/UK and Metric, rounded for convenience. Oven temperatures are provided in both Fahrenheit and Celsius.

1/4 teaspoon			1 ml
1/2 teaspoon			2 ml
1 teaspoon		1/3 tablespoon	5 ml
1 tablespoon	1/2 fluid ounce	3 teaspoons	15 ml
2 tablespoons	1 fluid ounce	1/8 cup	30 ml
1/4 cup	2 fluid ounces	4 tablespoons	60 ml
1/3 cup	2.6 fluid ounces	5 tablespoons + 1 teaspoon	80 ml
1/2 cup	4 fluid ounces	8 tablespoons	125 ml
3/4 cup	6 fluid ounces	12 tablespoons	180 ml
1 cup	8 fluid ounces	16 tablespoons	250 ml
2 cups	16 fluid ounces	32 tablespoons	500 ml
4 cups	32 fluid ounces		1 litre

Oven Temperatures

Fahrenheit	Celsius	Gas
250°	120°	1/2
275°	140°	1
300°	150°	2
325°	160°	3
350°	180°	4
375°	190°	5
400°	200°	6
425°	220°	7
450°	230°	8
475°	240°	9
500°	260°	10

1 ounce		30 grams
2 ounces		55 grams
3 ounces	1/4 pound	85 grams
4 ounces	1/2 pound	125 grams
8 ounces	3/4 pound	250 grams
12 ounces	1 pound	375 grams
16 ounces	2 pounds	454 grams
32 ounces		907 grams
35.2 ounces	2.2 pounds	1 kilogram

References

About Italian Food http://italianfood.about.com 2003.

Antrodoco Web www.paese.com/Antrodoco 2001.

BINNS, Brigit Legere. *Polenta*.
    San Francisco: Chronicle Books, 1997.

DANIELLE, Mario. *Mario's via Abruzzi: the cookbook*.
    New York: Mario's via Abruzzi, 2002.

FISHER, M.F.K *The Art of Eating*.
    Toronto: Random House of Canada, Ltd., 1976.

HAZAN, Marcella. *More Classic Italian Cooking*.
    New York: Ballantyne Books, 1984.

Lo PINTO, Maria. *The Art of Italian Cooking*.
    New York: Doubleday & Company, Inc., 1948.

NATALI, Carlo. *Abruzzi e Molise in Bocca*.
    Rimini: Edizione Gulliver, 2000.

ROOT, Waverley. *The Cooking of Italy*.
    New York: Time-Life Books, 1968.

ROOT, Waverley. *The Food of Italy*.
    New York: Vintage Books, May 1992.

SCICOLONE, Michele. *La Dolce Vita*.
    New York: William Morrow & Co., 1993.

Slow Food. www.slowfood.it and
    www.slowfood.com 2002.

TERRIGNO, Antonietta. *Italian Cooking:
    Great Classic Recipes*.
    Calgary: Osteria di Medici, 1999.

The Great Canadian Feast.
    Toronto: Key Porter Books Limited, 2002.

The Italian Trade Commission, New York
    www.italianmade.com December, 2002.

Trail Cooks Italian! Trail: Friends of Trail & District
    Public Library, 2001.

VISSER, Margaret *The Way We Are*.
    Toronto: Harper Collins Publishers Ltd., 1994.

WHITESIDE, Lorraine. *Healthy Mediterranean Cookery*.
    UK: Little, Brown, & Co., 1997.

Index

Recipes and Notes

Recipes and Notes

Recipes and Notes

Recipes and Notes

Recipes and Notes

....

....

....

....

....

....

....

....

....

....

....

....

....

....

....

Recipes and Notes